Marcia Hill
Editor

D0165101

Feminist Therapy as a Political Act

Feminist Therapy as a Political Act has been co-published simultaneously as *Women & Therapy*, Volume 21, Number 2 1998.

Pre-publication
REVIEWS,
COMMENTARIES,
EVALUATIONS . . .

"**T**his book is a valuable tool for feminist therapists and those who want to learn about feminist therapy. Marcia Hill has done an admirable job bringing together well-written articles by noted therapists dealing [with] the political nature of feminist therapy.

Bravo to Marcia Hill for producing this informative, thorough and readable volume. It is a real contribution to the field."

Florence L. Denmark, PhD
Robert S. Pace Distinguished
Professor of Psychology
Chair, Psychology Department

"**F**eminist Therapy as a Political Act is a provocative book. As a therapist and a feminist who has been in private practice for 16 years I have been through the changes in our field. This book is a reminder that therapy still needs feminist challenges. The same issues are clearly still with us: incest, gender bias, domestic violence, racism, homophobia and the institutional pathologizing of women's responses to all of the above. Even though we have indeed affected how the world works and thinks, there is more to do.

Feminist Therapy as a Political Act is a combination of revitalized theory and concrete suggestions of how to turn theory into action. It carries the reminder that contrary to the political messages of the last two decades the problems are still systemic and the solutions still need to be individual *and* collective.

I confess that I got a little defensive when one author discussed feminists' slide to accommodating managed care, something I have certainly done. On the more comfortable side, it is a relief to name that problem and move on to figuring out how to engage with the changes in health care. Both of my reactions, I think, are hallmarks of Feminist Therapy; risk being uncomfortable and work with colleagues and clients to address the problems. This book is an aid in both realms. Just in case we are not challenging ourselves in the midst of surviving the health care changes, *Feminist Therapy as a Political Act* reminds us. Just in case we have forgotten that we are in good company, *Feminist Therapy as a Political Act* reminds us of that, too."

G. Dorsey Green, PhD
Psychologist
Independent Practice

The Harrington Park Press

Feminist Therapy as a Political Act

Feminist Therapy as a Political Act has been co-published simultaneously as *Women & Therapy,* Volume 21, Number 2 1998.

Feminist Therapy
as a Political Act

Marcia Hill, EdD
Editor

Feminist Therapy as a Political Act, edited by Marcia Hill, was simultaneously issued by The Haworth Press, Inc., under the same title, as a special issue of the journal *Women & Therapy*, Volume 21, Number 2 1998, Marcia Hill and Esther D. Rothblum, Editors.

The Harrington Park Press
An Imprint of
The Haworth Press, Inc.
New York • London

1-56023-112-2

Published by

The Harrington Park Press, 10 Alice Street, Binghamton, NY 13904-1580 USA

The Harrington Park Press is an imprint of The Haworth Press, Inc., 10 Alice Street, Binghamton, NY 13904-1580 USA.

Feminist Therapy as a Political Act has been co-published simultaneously as *Women & Therapy,* Volume 21, Number 2 1998.

© 1998 by The Haworth Press, Inc. All rights reserved. No part of this work may be reproduced or utilized in any form or by any means, electronic or mechanical, including photocopying, microfilm and recording, or by any information storage and retrieval system, without permission in writing from the publisher. Printed in the United States of America.

The development, preparation, and publication of this work has been undertaken with great care. However, the publisher, employees, editors, and agents of The Haworth Press and all imprints of The Haworth Press, Inc., including The Haworth Medical Press and The Pharmaceutical Products Press, are not responsible for any errors contained herein or for consequences that may ensue from use of materials or information contained in this work. Opinions expressed by the author(s) are not necessarily those of The Haworth Press, Inc.

Cover design by Marylouise E. Doyle

Library of Congress Cataloging-in-Publication Data

Feminist therapy as a political act / Marcia Hill, editor.
      p. cm.
      ". . . co-published simultaneously as Women & therapy, volume 21, number 2, 1998."
      Includes bibliographical references and index.
      ISBN 0-7890-0517-4 (alk. paper) – ISBN 1-56023-112-2 (pbk.: alk. paper).
      1. Feminist therapy–Political aspects. 2. Psychotherapy. I. Hill, Marcia II. Women & therapy ; v. 21, no. 2.
RC489.F45F456 1998
616.89′14′082–dc21
                                           98-12812
                                               CIP

INDEXING & ABSTRACTING

Contributions to this publication are selectively indexed or abstracted in print, electronic, online, or CD-ROM version(s) of the reference tools and information services listed below. This list is current as of the copyright date of this publication. See the end of this section for additional notes.

- *Abstracts of Research in Pastoral Care & Counseling*, Loyola College, 7135 Minstrel Way, Suite 101, Columbia, MD 21045

- *Academic Abstracts/CD-ROM,* EBSCO Publishing Editorial Department, P.O. Box 590, Ipswich, MA 01938-0590

- *Academic Index (on-line)*, Information Access Company, 362 Lakeside Drive, Foster City, CA 94404

- *Alternative Press Index*, Alternative Press Center, Inc., P.O. Box 33109, Baltimore, MD 21218-0401

- *Behavioral Medicine Abstracts*, University of Washington, Department of Social Work & Speech & Hearing Sciences, Box 354900, Seattle, WA 98195

- *CNPIEC Reference Guide: Chinese National Directory of Foreign Periodicals*, P.O. Box 88, Beijing, People's Republic of China

- *Current Contents: Clinical Medicine/Life Sciences (CC: CM/LS) (weekly Table of Contents Service), and Social Science Citation Index. Articles also searchable through Social SciSearch, ISI's online database and in ISI's Research Alert current awareness service,* Institute for Scientific Information, 3501 Market Street, Philadelphia, PA 19104-3302 (USA)

- *Digest of Neurology and Psychiatry*, The Institute of Living, 400 Washington Street, Hartford, CT 06106

- *Expanded Academic Index,* Information Access Company, 362 Lakeside Drive, Forest City, CA 94404

- *Family Studies Database (online and CD/ROM),* National Information Services Corporation, 306 East Baltimore Pike, 2nd Floor, Media, PA 19063

(continued)

- *Family Violence & Sexual Assault Bulletin*, Family Violence & Sexual Assault Institute, 1121 E. South East Loop 323, Suite 130, Tyler, TX 75701

- *Feminist Periodicals: A Current Listing of Contents*, Women's Studies Librarian-at-Large, 728 State Street, 430 Memorial Library, Madison, WI 53706

- *Health Source: Indexing & Abstracting of 160 selected health related journals, updated monthly:* EBSCO Publishing, 83 Pine Street, Peabody, MA 01960

- *Health Source Plus: expanded version of "Health Source" to be released shortly:* EBSCO Publishing, 83 Pine Street, Peabody, MA 01960

- *Higher Education Abstracts*, Claremont Graduate University, 231 East Tenth Street, Claremont, CA 91711

- *IBZ International Bibliography of Periodical Literature*, Zeller Verlag GmbH & Co., P.O.B. 1949, d-49009, Osnabruck, Germany

- *Index to Periodical Articles Related to Law*, University of Texas, 727 East 26th Street, Austin, TX 78705

- *INTERNET ACCESS (& additional networks) Bulletin Board for Libraries ("BUBL") coverage of information resources on INTERNET, JANET, and other networks.*
  - <URL:http://bubl.ac.uk/>
  - The new locations will be found under <URL:http://bubl.ac.uk/link/>.
  - Any existing BUBL users who have problems finding information on the new service should contact the BUBL help line by sending e-mail to <bubl@bubl.ac.uk>.

  The Andersonian Library, Curran Building, 101 St. James Road, Glasgow G4 0NS, Scotland

- *Mental Health Abstracts (online through DIALOG)*, IFI/Plenum Data Company, 3202 Kirkwood Highway, Wilmington, DE 19808

- *ONS Nursing Scan in Oncology-NAACOG's Women's Health Nursing Scan*, NURSECOM, Inc., 1211 Locust Street, Philadelphia, PA 19107

(continued)

- *PASCAL, c/o Institute de L'Information Scientifique et Technique. Cross-disciplinary electronic database covering the fields of science, technology & medicine.* Also available on CD-ROM, and can generate customized retrospective searches. For more information: INIST, Customer Desk, 2, allee du Parc de Brabois, F-54514 Vandoeuvre Cedex, France; http//www.inist.fr

- *Periodical Abstracts, Research I* (general & basic reference indexing & abstracting data-base from University Microfilms International (UMI), 300 North Zeeb Road, P.O. Box 1346, Ann Arbor, MI 48106-1346), UMI Data Courier, P.O. Box 32770, Louisville, KY 40232-2770

- *Periodical Abstracts, Research II* (broad coverage indexing & abstracting data-base from University Microfilms International (UMI), 300 North Zeeb Road, P.O. Box 1346, Ann Arbor, MI 48106-1346), UMI Data Courier, P.O. Box 32770, Louisville, KY 40232-2770

- *Psychological Abstracts (PsycINFO)*, American Psychological Association, P.O. Box 91600, Washington, DC 20090-1600

- *Published International Literature on Traumatic Stress (The PILOTS Database)*, National Center for Post-Traumatic Stress Disorder (116 D), VA Medical Center, White River Junction, VT 05009

- *Sage Family Studies Abstracts (SFSA)*, Sage Publications, Inc., 2455 Teller Road, Newbury Park, CA 91320

- *Social Work Abstracts*, National Association of Social Workers, 750 First Street NW, 8th Floor, Washington, DC 20002

- *Sociological Abstracts (SA),* Sociological Abstracts, Inc., P.O. Box 22206, San Diego, CA 92192-0206

- *Studies on Women Abstracts*, Carfax Publishing Company, P.O. Box 25, Abingdon, Oxon OX14 3UE, United Kingdom

- *Violence and Abuse Abstracts: A Review of Current Literature on Interpersonal Violence (VAA)*, Sage Publications, Inc., 2455 Teller Road, Newbury Park, CA 91320

- *Women "R" CD/ROM*, Softline Information, Inc., 20 Summer Street, Stamford, CT 06901

- *Women Studies Abstracts*, Rush Publishing Company, P.O. Box 1, Rush, NY 14543

- *Women's Studies Index (indexed comprehensively)*, G. K. Hall & Co., P.O. Box 159, Thorndike, ME 04986

(continued)

SPECIAL BIBLIOGRAPHIC NOTES

related to special journal issues (separates)
and indexing/abstracting

❑ indexing/abstracting services in this list will also cover material in any "separate" that is co-published simultaneously with Haworth's special thematic journal issue or DocuSerial. Indexing/abstracting usually covers material at the article/chapter level.

❑ monographic co-editions are intended for either non-subscribers or libraries which intend to purchase a second copy for their circulating collections.

❑ monographic co-editions are reported to all jobbers/wholesalers/approval plans. The source journal is listed as the "series" to assist the prevention of duplicate purchasing in the same manner utilized for books-in-series.

❑ to facilitate user/access services all indexing/abstracting services are encouraged to utilize the co-indexing entry note indicated at the bottom of the first page of each article/chapter/contribution.

❑ this is intended to assist a library user of any reference tool (whether print, electronic, online, or CD-ROM) to locate the monographic version if the library has purchased this version but not a subscription to the source journal.

❑ individual articles/chapters in any Haworth publication are also available through the Haworth Document Delivery Service (HDDS).

CONTENTS

ABOUT THE EDITOR

Marcia Hill, EdD, is a psychologist who has spent over 20 years practicing psychotherapy. She is Co-Editor of the journal *Women & Therapy* and a member and past Chair of the Feminist Therapy Institute. In addition to therapy, Dr. Hill does occasional teaching, writing, and consulting in the areas of feminist therapy theory and practice. The Editor of *More than a Mirror: How Clients Influence Therapists' Lives* (The Haworth Press, Inc., 1997), she has co-edited four other Haworth books: *Classism and Feminist Therapy: Counting Costs* (1996); *Couples Therapy: Feminist Perspectives* (1996); *Children's Rights, Therapists' Responsibilities: Feminist Commentaries* (1997); and *Breaking the Rules: Women in Prison and Feminist Therapy* (1998). She is currently in private practice in Montpelier, Vermont.

ALL HARRINGTON PARK PRESS BOOKS
ARE PRINTED ON CERTIFIED
ACID-FREE PAPER

Preface

Recently there has been a certain amount of handwringing among some critics of feminist therapy, wondering whether the practice of feminist therapy has been losing its grounding in political awareness. I have been curious about the meaning of this discourse. Is it a form of backlash, not unlike the media glee in announcing that feminism was dead? Does it represent a longing for what some imagine were simpler times, with simpler political analyses unsullied by the demands of practicing as a therapist in the late 1990s? Politics, as Mary Ballou and I point out in the article that opens this compilation, assumes various guises, is understood and practiced differently depending on the location of the individual. Politics enacted by the therapist is not the same as politics enacted by the academic or the community organizer or the businesswoman. Yet, each may be able to articulate a political analysis that informs her choices and constructs her work.

Rather than assuming the political state of feminist therapy, we begin this collection by examining what experienced feminist therapists themselves say about how they integrate politics into their work (Hill and Ballou). The results indicate a rich variety of ways that these practitioners politicize the therapy relationship, setting, assumptions, techniques and dialogue. This is followed by Jeanne Marecek and Diane Kravetz's detailed analysis of the language used by three diverse feminist therapists to describe their work. They highlight the way that patterns of speech and conceptualization emphasize some aspects of power while concealing others.

Having considered feminist therapy politics both through language and behavior, we next turn to models of political thinking in the context of therapy. Susan Morrow and Donna Hawxhurst offer a framework for political analysis in therapy, looking at the conditions and dimensions of

[Haworth co-indexing entry note]: "Preface." Hill, Marcia. Co-published simultaneously in *Women & Therapy* (The Haworth Press, Inc.) Vol. 21, No. 2, 1998, pp. xvii-xix; and: *Feminist Therapy as a Political Act* (ed: Marcia Hill) The Haworth Press, Inc., 1998, pp. xv-xvii; and: *Feminist Therapy as a Political Act* (ed: Marcia Hill) The Harrington Park Press, an imprint of The Haworth Press, Inc., 1998, pp. xiii-xv. Single or multiple copies of this article are available for a fee from The Haworth Document Delivery Service [1-800-342-9678, 9:00 a.m. - 5:00 p.m. (EST). E-mail address: getinfo@haworth.com].

© 1998 by The Haworth Press, Inc. All rights reserved. *xiii* empowerment. Susan Barrett explains the multifaceted construct of personal identity. She moves beyond identity politics, demonstrating that identity is a complex combination of minority and dominant positions, group membership and individual sense of self. These two theoretical pieces are followed by Masami Matsuyuki's presentation of the evolution and practice of feminist counseling in Japan. Both the similarities and differences in relation to feminist therapy in the United States are instructive.

But what does all of this mean in the varied settings in which feminist therapy is practiced? Turning to the specific, we then look at three very different applications of feminist therapy politics. Jo Oppenheimer describes how survivors of incest and sexual abuse "went public" in Israel through art, poetry, videos, performances and panels: a powerful political action. Two feminist therapists (Nayyar Javed and Nikki Gerrard) exchange letters about working with men, weaving the complications of race and being mothers of sons into their thinking. And Renée Spencer details for the reader the challenges and rewards of constructing a hospital program based on the principles of the Stone Center work.

Finally, we close this volume with Kayla Weiner's call for undisguised political action as a part of therapy. She considers it the responsibility of all people to change the world for the better and challenges both therapists and clients to do so as part of being a fully functioning person.

Many years ago, I was harassed on the street by some young men in a truck stopped at a traffic light. It was the middle of the day with plenty of people around and, feeling relatively safe in my small town, I elected to confront the sexist behavior. I marched up to the truck and demanded, "Do you know how that feels? Would you want to be treated that way? Well, think about it!" The light changed and they drove off; I walked on, somewhat shaken but pleased. Years later, a therapist I was supervising told me about a dream a client of hers had, a woman who had a history of sexual abuse. I was in the dream, obviously a symbol of this client's own potential for power and change. The woman had been one of the witnesses to my confrontation all those years ago, and had remembered and used my small political act when she needed it. I still don't know who this woman is; I never imagined that I had affected anyone beyond (I hoped!) the men in the car.

Kayla Weiner, in this volume, notes that "each individual must realize that every action . . . has a ripple effect and makes a political statement . . ." In therapy, it is easy to lose track of the ripple effect of our choices. We see people for a while and they go on with their lives, and we don't always know what they do or dream years later. But be assured that someone whose therapy is collaborative will come to expect respect; someone whose pain is put in a larger context will not forget that context. Feminist therapists create revolution insidiously, one person at a time. I hope that this volume both inspires and supports your own revolution.

Marcia Hill

Making Therapy Feminist:
A Practice Survey

Marcia Hill
Mary Ballou

SUMMARY. The authors wished to gather information about the ways in which experienced feminist therapists are integrating the principles of feminist therapy into their practice. Two areas of interest were examined: the application of specific therapy techniques and the ongoing background dialogue of therapy. A survey asking two open-ended questions regarding these areas was mailed to members of the Feminist Therapy Institute. Responses were organized into categories based on feminist therapy principles for which there was consensus in the literature and as described in the Feminist Therapy Code of Ethics.

Results showed strong support for a variety of ways on which feminist therapists enact these principles, with particular attention given by respondents to power in the structure and relationship of therapy. Respondents also described creative ways in which they had modified cognitive-behavioral, hypnosis, and other therapy techniques in order to make them more compatible with feminist principles. *[Article copies available for a fee from The Haworth Document Delivery Service: 1-800-342-9678. E-mail address: getinfo@haworth.com]*

Mary Ballou, PhD, is an academic at Northeastern University and a practitioner. Marcia Hill, EdD, is a psychologist in private practice and co-editor of *Women & Therapy.*

This work was a collaborative effort. The authors thank Anat Hampel and Maria Dobbins for their generous assistance.

Address correspondence to: Mary Ballou, Dept. of Counseling Psychology, 203 Lake Hall, Northeastern University, Boston, MA 02115.

[Haworth co-indexing entry note]: "Making Therapy Feminist: A Practice Survey." Hill, Marcia, and Mary Ballou. Co-published simultaneously in *Women & Therapy* (The Haworth Press, Inc.) Vol. 21, No. 2, 1998, pp. 1-16; and: *Feminist Therapy as a Political Act* (ed: Marcia Hill) The Haworth Press, Inc., 1998, pp. 1-16; and: *Feminist Therapy as a Political Act* (ed: Marcia Hill) The Harrington Park Press, an imprint of The Haworth Press, Inc., 1998, pp. 1-16. Single or multiple copies of this article are available for a fee from The Haworth Document Delivery Service [1-800-342-9678, 9:00 a.m. - 5:00 p.m. (EST). E-mail address: getinfo@haworth.com].

© 1998 by The Haworth Press, Inc. All rights reserved.

Theory, research and practice in feminist therapy has matured significantly in the past two decades. In this time, the field has gone from its beginnings in the radical idea that therapy itself had political implications to an increasingly complex theorizing of the tenets of feminist therapy practice. More recently, the integration of our understanding of the effects of race, class, sexual orientation and other dimensions of power and privilege has enriched feminist therapy theory. The next step for feminist therapy is a fuller articulation of the lived enactment of feminist therapy, the "how to" of practice. What follows is an extension of that dialogue.

"Feminist therapy as it exists is a philosophy of psychotherapy, not a prescription or technique" (Brodsky, 1992, p. 51). Indeed, the majority of the discourse to date has focused on formulating a consensus about the general themes or elements of feminist therapy. At this point, there is substantial agreement in the literature about the principles of feminist therapy. These are:

1. Feminist therapy is based in valuing women's experience; "the personal is political" (Ballou, 1995; Brown, 1994; Enns, 1993; Gilbert, 1980; Hill, 1990; Kaschak, 1981, 1992; Lerman, 1986; Worell & Remer, 1992). This principle has evolved out of the consciousness-raising groups in the beginning of the second wave of the women's movement. Feminists found that "reality" had been constructed based largely on the experiences of men (particularly white, heterosexual, middle-class men) (Frye, 1983) and that much could be learned about the truth of women's experience from women themselves. In later work (Brown & Ballou, 1992), the inverse–"the political is personal"–was used to capture the influence of structural and sociocultural factors on the psychological.

2. Feminist therapy recognizes that much of the distress that brings people to therapy is socioculturally based (Ballou, 1990, 1995; Ballou & Gabalac, 1985; Brown, 1990; Brown and Brodsky, 1992; Comas-Diaz, 1987, 1991; Kaschak, 1981, 1992; Rawlings & Carter, 1977; Worell & Remer, 1992). Brown and Brodsky (1992) describe this as seeing the goals of therapy as including a changed perspective on the sociocultural realities that affect the client's life. Comas-Diaz (1987, 1991) suggests that therapy should clarify interactions between the client's social environment and internal experience. Others (Brown, 1990; Rawlings & Carter 1977; Worell & Remer, 1992) emphasize that gender role analysis is central to understanding the client's distress. These are all ways of saying that women's pain cannot be understood outside of the context of women's oppression. Oliva Espin states directly that "a therapist who does not

have an analysis of the social world could not be a good therapist" (1994, p. 283).

3. Feminist therapists attend to power in the therapy relationship, with the goal of developing more egalitarian structures and relationships in therapy (Ballou, 1990, 1995; Ballou & Gabalac, 1985; Brown, 1994; Enns, 1993; Feminist Therapy Institute, 1990; Gilbert, 1980; Hill, 1992; Jordan, Kaplan, Miller, Stiver, & Surrey, 1991; Worell & Remer, 1992). This element is a predictable outcome of understanding the ways in which misuse of power has been destructive to women. How can the therapist, who by virtue of her role has greater power than the client, avoid replicating the very situation which has hurt the client in the first place? Feminist therapists thus emphasize an "ethic of respect" (Hill, 1990, p. 56), which includes practices such as working collaboratively with the client, making the therapist's values explicit, etc.

4. Feminist therapists have an integrated analysis of oppression; i.e., they understand the ways in which race/ethnicity, sexual orientation, class, religion, size, dis/ability and age are an integral part of each client's experience in addition to gender (Brown & Ballou, 1992; Brown, 1994; Brown & Brodsky, 1992; Comas-Diaz, 1987, 1991; Espin & Gawelek, 1992; Feminist Therapy Institute, 1990; Hammond, 1987; Kanuha, 1990; Kaschak, 1992; Lerman, 1986). In perhaps the last ten years, feminist therapy has evolved a more complex analysis of oppression and an awareness that gender cannot be separated from other ways in which a culture stratifies human difference, privileging some at the expense of others. Turner (1991) describes this as how the client negotiates and copes with multiple cultural worlds.

5. The ultimate intention of feminist therapy is to create social change (Ballou, 1990, 1995; Ballou & Gabalac, 1985; Brown, 1994; Enns, 1992; Feminist Therapy Institute, 1990; Greenspan, 1983; Whalen, 1996). Feminist therapists see themselves as working for change on an individual level, by practicing a therapy that creates both an awareness of sociocultural inequities and an alternative experience for the client. Feminist therapists also see direct action for social change as part of their responsibility *as therapists* (Feminist Therapy Institute, 1990).

In the emphasis on developing principles and theory, feminist therapists have had considerably less to say about the concrete practice of feminist therapy. Partly this is because feminist therapy, in contrast to many other therapies (gestalt, cognitive-behavioral, rational-emotive, etc.) is value-driven rather than technique-driven. In fact, "feminist therapists may practice in a variety of modalities" (Brodsky, 1980). The principles and philosophy of feminist therapy have been integrated into a range of techniques and schools of thought, including psychodynamic, behavioral, experiential, and many others (Kaschak, 1992; Rothblum & Cole, 1986).

There is strong consensus among feminist therapists about some of the structural elements of the therapy situation itself. By "structural elements" we mean how fees are negotiated, how client problems are named or "diagnosed," strategies for demystifying therapy and removing victim blame, and other similar elements. In general, feminist therapists have restructured the practice of therapy to return power to the client as much as is practical (Ballou & Gabalac, 1985; Brown, 1994; Hill, 1992; Kaschak, 1992; Rosewater & Walker, 1985). In addition, a number of authors describe the use of sex-role analysis, which is a technique unique to feminist therapy (Kaschak, 1981; Williams, 1976; Worell & Remer, 1992).

However, we would differentiate the use of sex-role analysis and changes in structural elements of therapy from the integration of feminist values into the use of other therapy techniques as well as into the general ongoing dialogue of therapy. The particulars of this integration have largely remained hidden, at least as far as the literature goes. To some extent, this is a reflection of the difficulty in articulating what is often a subtle difference in approach between, say, a feminist hypnotist and a mainstream hypnotist, or a feminist behaviorist and a more traditional one. Deborah Leupnitz says,

> Feminism is not a set of therapeutic techniques but a sensibility, a political and aesthetic center that informs a work pervasively. One does not merely make clinical interventions in the family as a feminist; one also greets the family and sets the fee as a feminist. The words spoken during a session that catch one's attention or that slip by, the things that make one feel warm toward the family, and the things that offend are all determined in part by this sensibility. (1988, p. 231)

Articulating these kinds of subtleties is daunting. However, difficulties in description do not mean that all description is impossible. In an effort to discover the specifics of what therapists do in their practice of therapy that is explicitly feminist, the authors chose the direct approach: ask feminist therapists.

In considering the application of feminist principles in the practice of psychotherapy, we would like to make a distinction between what might be considered "surface" as opposed to "deep" integration. "Surface" or liberal, gender-aware practice has already made a significant impact on mainstream practice. The 1992 revision of the American Psychological Association's code of ethics, for example, includes far greater attention to matters of sexual exploitation than previous codes, as well as mandating responsibility for cultural and gender literacy on the part of the therapist. Both of these elements indicate feminist influence; indeed, when drafting the ethics code, APA sought consultation from state committees on women and on ethnic minorities.

Understanding rape as an act of male violence, recognizing the frequency and destructiveness of childhood sexual abuse, and appreciating the consequences of domestic violence all are instances of perspectives that were considered radical when first introduced by feminists. Now all are fairly well integrated, at least superficially, into everyday practice by most therapists, even those who would not consider themselves feminist. The current emphasis on consumer rights in therapy has certainly been influenced by feminist critiques of various practices that mystified therapy and infantilized the client. And a number of recently popular schools of therapeutic thought, most notable among them narrative therapy (as originally presented, e.g., White & Epston, 1990), owe a huge intellectual debt to twenty-five years of writing and thinking in which feminist therapists have emphasized externalization of problems and collaboration with the client.

What is perhaps most striking about all of these examples of the influence of feminism on today's mainstream therapy practices is that the feminist scholarship behind them remains almost entirely unacknowledged. This is a very revealing state of affairs for a branch of social science that emphasizes research and citation of prior work as central to its methodology. Perhaps mainstream psychotherapy is willing to borrow what is useful from feminist work, so long as the concepts are not acknowledged to be feminist in origin. While imitation may be the most sincere form of flattery, this amounts to intellectual plagiarism. It speaks volumes about how dangerous and unacceptable feminism continues to be, and implies recognition of the truly radical nature of feminist thought.

Much less has been done about what we might call the "deep" integration of feminist principles into the practice of therapy, that is, the ways in which feminists change the practice of therapy itself. Feminist therapy is not traditional therapy with gender awareness added; it is a complete transformation of the way in which therapy is understood and practiced. There have been very few descriptions of how feminism is used to transform a specific therapeutic strategy. Webster (1995) describes the feminist application of solution-focused practices, and Hill (1992) presents a feminist reworking of paradoxical techniques. Explanations as to how feminism is integrated into the ongoing dialogue of therapy are limited, but somewhat more available. Worell and Remer (1992), Brown (1994) and Kaschak (1992) give numerous examples of feminist thinking and interventions in the context of particular cases, and Laura Brown demonstrates feminist therapy on videotape for the APA series showing various systems of psychotherapy (1994). A casebook of ethical decision-making (Rave & Larsen, 1995) offers the responses of many feminist therapists to a wide range of ethical dilemmas. The intent of the current study is to add to those descriptions, both of the therapy dialogue in general and how specific therapeutic strategies are made feminist.

METHOD

Our concern is how feminist politics are made real through the current practice of feminist therapy. What are the ways in which the principles of feminist therapy get enacted in the therapy session? How do feminist therapists do the everyday practice of therapy differently from mainstream therapists? In particular, how do feminist therapists adapt specific therapeutic strategies and what happens in the ongoing background dialogue of feminist therapy?

We asked members of the Feminist Therapy Institute for examples of feminist therapy practice. Categories for organizing their responses were drawn from the principles of feminist therapy and from the feminist therapy code of ethics, which were combined in order to reduce overlap. We used a grounded theory analysis, meaning that the content analysis of the responses was based in these feminist principles.

Respondents were limited to members of the Feminist Therapy Institute. The Institute's membership is characterized by: commitment to the development of feminist therapy theory and practice, a multicultural and anti-racist perspective in all areas of feminist therapy, challenging and being challenged by work in progress and broadening perspectives, and amplifying personal and professional visions of what feminist therapy can be and become (drawn from the organizational brochure). Members must have worked as feminist therapists for at least five years and must sign the feminist ethical guidelines. Membership includes women with ages ranging from 30s to 80s, and living mostly in the U.S., although a few members live in Canada, Europe, South Africa and Israel. Their length of practice as feminist therapists ranges from eight years to over twenty. Women from a variety of community-based and professional backgrounds are members and they work in settings across the spectrum. The membership is female, predominantly European descent, and primarily middle and upper middle class by profession. This particular group of feminist therapists was selected because the membership criteria well suited the needs of the study. The authors are also members and have held leadership positions in the group; we hoped that our involvement might encourage thoughtful participation.

We mailed an explanation of our intent and two open-ended questions, requesting reflective examples, rather than a summative accounting, of respondents' practice in two broad areas of therapy.

The first survey question was: "Have you adapted a specific therapeutic strategy so that it is feminist? By specific strategy we mean such things as hypnosis, EMDR, cognitive-behavioral techniques, etc. Please describe in some detail how you have made the technique more feminist. For example, Marcia uses paradox by explaining to the client how it works, why it might be helpful, and then inviting the client to help construct the paradoxical idea or activity."

The second survey question was: "Please describe one or more examples of ways that you make the substance or ongoing dialogue of therapy feminist. By 'ongoing dialogue' we mean such things as discussing a dream, deciding the focus of the work, terminating therapy, conveying empathy, conceptualizing and using the relationship with the client, etc. (We are intentionally omitting what we think of as the structural elements of therapy, such as choosing a diagnosis, setting fees, or preparing reports, as we believe these elements are already somewhat addressed in the literature.) For example, Mary asks her clients the classic question of political analysis, 'Who benefits from your actions?' or will notice limiting beliefs that may have to do with gender expectations and ask the client 'Where did you learn that?'."

The questionnaire was mailed to 125 active members of the Feminist Therapy Institute. A response time of two-and-a-half weeks was allowed; three weeks later a reminder e-mail or phone call was made.

A matrix of coding categories was developed to assist in organizing the responses. These were drawn from both the consensual literature, discussed earlier in this paper, and from the code of ethics for feminist therapists (Lerman & Porter, 1990), which was also developed consensually by feminist therapists. The conceptual overlap between the two sets of principles was reduced, leaving five general categories. These were:

1. based in valuing women's experience
2. recognition of the sociocultural causes of distress
3. attention to power in therapy
4. an integrated analysis of oppression
5. goal of social change

We used these theoretical points as a basis for our data organization for two reasons. First, they are definitional and consensual among feminist therapists. And second, because they form a foundation for thinking about feminist therapy, they provide a platform from which to view changes and developments that may have occurred in the practice of feminist therapy over time. Two trained doctoral students coded the responses of each participant into these categories; some responses fit into more than one category. Their work was checked for accuracy and intercoder consistency. The results, which organized each respondent's reflections upon her own practice experiences, formed the basis for our analysis.

This methodology makes use of the experience, reflection and creativity of this group of advanced and committed feminist therapists. The material generated was organized into categories chosen because they were grounded in consensually developed feminist therapy principles. We used these findings to engage in a "dialectical process" (Henwood & Pidgen, 1995) between the respondents and the researchers. Our intent was to use the results to extend and deepen the understanding of how the practice of feminist therapy has evolved over time.

RESULTS AND DISCUSSION

This survey asked for information in two areas of therapy: the application of technique and what we called the "ongoing dialogue" of therapy. We asked respondents for examples of ways in which they implemented feminist therapy, with the goal of developing a more in-depth picture of the actual practice of feminist therapy. We wanted information about practitioners' subtle choices and developments in the practice of feminist therapy. It is important to note that respondents were not asked to give a complete or exhaustive accounting of the elements of feminist therapy or of all the techniques that they made use of. These results must therefore be seen as an initial description of some, but not all, of the ways that feminist therapy is implemented.

A total of 45 responses was received, out of 125 sent. This represents a response rate of 36 percent. Of these, 10 indicated reasons they were unable to participate, leaving 35 usable responses. We asked practitioners to describe how they practiced feminist therapy; we did not structure their responses beyond requesting that they speak to our two general areas of interest. Most of the responses addressed matters concerning the ongoing dialogue of therapy, with fewer describing specific feminist adaptations of therapy techniques. We will look first at responses that discuss the general practice of therapy, and then at technique.

The Ongoing Dialogue of Therapy

Power Differentials, Overlapping Relationships, and Therapist Accountability

The great majority of comments concerned ways of making therapy more responsive to matters of power. In fact, virtually every participant discussed sensitivity to power in the structure and relationship of therapy. Respondents described a wide variety of ways of sharing power with the client and insuring that the power available to the therapist by virtue of her role would be contained and limited.

A number of therapists mentioned ways of giving the client information, both about the therapy process and about specific therapy techniques. "[I] give the client a whole lot more information than most nonfeminist therapists do," was how Sue Morrow put it. Susan Barrett described offering clients "mini teaching sessions" about the therapy process, and others give similar descriptions of what has commonly been called "demystifying therapy." A basic tenet of feminist therapy is that therapy is never value-neutral, as Bella Savrin notes in her response. The therapists in this survey take seriously their responsibility for being explicit about the values they bring to the work. Therapist accountability to the client is a repeated theme. Some therapists give clients information concretely, through handouts explaining how therapy works and client rights. Ruth Parvin gives a client information before the first meeting about how to confront the therapist with any concerns about therapy, and others also state that they invite client feedback and questions about the work. Several therapists have a lending library so that clients have access to written information about areas of interest.

In addition to accountability in terms of responsiveness to client feedback, some therapists specifically mentioned seeking out consultation or made more general statements about the importance of practicing ethically and competently. Sue Morrow writes in some detail about discussing overlapping relationships with all clients at the beginning of therapy.

A collaborative stance is mentioned almost universally. Respondents describe setting goals, developing homework assignments, assessing progress, and deciding about termination jointly with the client. The respondents describe an emphasis on client, as opposed to therapist expertise: "I do not believe that I know more than you about you" (Jo Romaniello). Sandra Vedovato opens sessions by reviewing her progress notes from the previous session with the client. Judicious use of self-disclosure is advocated by some respondents who see this as one tool to help "strip away the shame" (Gail Anderson) of certain experiences or to present the therapist as, like the client, a feeling and flawed human. This stance can be expensive for the therapist, as Elizabeth Reed notes: " . . . some of the feminist infusion into the therapy process is uncomfortable *for me*. The patriarchal model of therapist as authority in the desk chair behind a closed door is easier on the therapist" (emphasis in the original).

Sociocultural Causes of Distress

Recognition of the external, i.e., sociocultural and structural, causes of much client distress is a hallmark of feminist therapy; it is the second most frequent topic of discussion (after power) for our respondents. Gail Pheterson puts it elegantly: "I try to distinguish *social defense*, i.e., resistance against current oppression, from *psychic defense*, i.e., resistance against recognition of reality due to past trauma" (emphasis in the original). She elaborates that "therapists ungrounded in feminist theory and practice are prone to misinterpret social resistance as psychic resistance, thereby discounting women's perceptions of injustice and undermining their sense of personal integrity."

Many respondents either ask clients explicitly about the influence of gender on their experiences and perceived choices, or filter what clients say through the lens of gender inequities. Virtually all discuss the impact of gender bias on their clients' concerns when appropriate. Therapists describe consideration of gender oppression as a factor in self-statements, internalized beliefs, self-blame and self-hatred, socialization influences and obstacles to change. Some specifically mention using other cultural lenses such as race/ethnicity, class and sexual orientation, in addition to gender, with which to understand clients' experiences of oppression. These will be discussed further in the section on an integrated analysis of oppression. There is a repeated suggestion of the intertwined nature of internally and externally caused distress, with an emphasis on the importance of recognizing the external. Elizabeth Reed says simply and directly, "There is suffering from unfair treatment in the world."

Valuing Women's Experience

Although difficult to describe, many respondents nonetheless focused on ways that they prioritize and honor the reality of their clients. "I stay with the client's sense of what is true," is how one anonymous writer put it. Phyllis Perry states, "She [the client] knows her own mind, heart and soul." Others take a slightly different perspective, and talk instead about the ways in which they incorporate into the therapy an understanding about experiences common to many women, such as women's difficulties with subordinating their needs to others (Rebecca Allen), women's need to feel agency in their own lives (Joyce Warshow), or women's disconnection from their bodies (Anonymous).

Integrated Analysis of Oppression

A number of participants' responses indicate a view of oppression as multifaceted and interlocking, with gender oppression being one of several elements. Gail Anderson describes in detail the use of dolls with varying skin colors in play therapy, and the ways in which she uses them to counteract racism. An anonymous respondent mentions her attention to diversity (racial, socioeconomic and sexual orientation) in group therapy. Others simply subsume a range of oppressions under the rubric of "cultural" influences. There are a number of particular references to efforts to be sensitive to differences, with race/ethnicity, sexual orientation, socioeconomic class and body size mentioned specifically.

Social Change

These therapists describe working for social change in both subtle and overt ways. Subtle ways include such areas as assumptions made and not made about clients' lives, goals of therapy, and even choices of magazines and artwork. For example, Ruth Parvin refuses to put what she calls "body impossibility" magazines in her waiting room. Others mention not making assumptions about the nature of the client's close relationships (i.e., sex of partner, how the client defines her "family," etc.). Elizabeth Reed intentionally makes certain assumptions as a method of encouraging change: that there is equal responsibility for home and child rearing between partners, with unequal treatment the exception.

Others are more overt about working for social change. Jo Romaniello advocates directly for her clients, as does Gail Anderson. Gail also describes teaching children how to advocate for themselves and states that she considers political action part of treatment planning.

Specific Treatment Strategies

Respondents describe selecting the tools they use based on compatibility with feminist principles. Thus, some state that they are uncomfortable using hypnosis, for example, because it seems too focused on therapist control. Others take particular strategies and adapt them to be more in line with feminist principles of minimizing power differentials, valuing women's experience, recognizing the impact of oppression on clients' experience, and so forth. Bella Savrin may be speaking for many when she says that she adapts all tools to be more feminist.

Cognitive-Behavioral Therapy

Participants focus particularly on collaboration with the client, such as inviting the client to set goals for change. Sandra Coffman looks at whether the client's cognitive beliefs were learned in response to cultural and gender expectations. Doris Howard asks, "What do you get out of this?," "What does the other get out of this?," and "Are these equal?" in order to reveal underlying inequalities. Gail Anderson discusses specific ways that clients can challenge self-blaming beliefs about sexual abuse. Marcia Hill introduces cognitive techniques to clients by using their experiences with unlearning prejudice as an example of ways they may already know how to challenge destructive beliefs.

Hypnosis

Several respondents make a point of presenting hypnosis as a skill under the client's control, and then teaching self-hypnosis skills to the client. Denny Webster uses a particular hypnotic protocol in which she asks for explicit permission with each step of the process.

Other Techniques

A number of other feminist adaptations of technique were mentioned briefly, usually by just one respondent. Elizabeth Reed articulates the sexist and heterosexist biases in Jungian and other standard methods of dream analysis, suggesting alternatives to the client. Gail Anderson makes play therapy feminist by integration of attention to race, gender, and a variety of ways of giving the child power. Acknowledging the importance of relationship in the DESC scripting technique and using female developmental theory were both mentioned by Carolyn Larsen. Denny Webster has specific strategies to assist women in focusing on self-care; Carol Cotton has developed ways for women to "name and . . . release the impact of patriarchal values." Reframing the analytic symbol of the penis to one of male power is described by Joyce Warshow. Jan Litwack has evolved a structured autobiography as a way for clients to describe their world. And both Bella Savrin and Marcia Hill teach clients paradoxical techniques for their own use.

CONCLUSIONS

This study has been an effort to move beyond the basics of practice in feminist therapy to a more elaborated understanding of how feminist therapy theory is being enacted. The consensus that has developed in the literature about the principles of feminist therapy–valuing women's experience, the sociocultural basis of distress, attention to power in the therapy relationship, an integrated analysis of oppression, and the goal of creating social change–has, we noted, also developed in the daily practice of feminist therapists. In addition, feminist therapists are selecting, inventing, and making creative adaptations of existing therapy techniques in order to bring these more in line with a feminist philosophy of treatment.

Our method was based in a grounded theory analysis of the responses received, which then formed the basis for a dialectical process between the participants and the researchers. This method also paralleled what feminist therapists are doing in their work: valuing the experiences of women, we asked open-ended questions in order to collect and listen to the lived experience of clinicians. It parallels, also, the method of consciousness-raising groups. C-R groups, because the previous database about women was contaminated by having originated in a patriarchal culture, turned to women's descriptions of their own lives for the elements of a more accurate picture of women's reality. Some of the literature about therapy practice has been similarly contaminated and we have thus turned to feminist therapists' own descriptions of their work for a picture with more accuracy and depth.

These descriptions might provide a start toward building a consensual understanding of the more embedded or nuanced ways that feminist theory is translated into feminist therapy practice. Any one participant response may represent a unique adaptation of feminist principles or may be an indicator of what virtually every feminist therapist is doing but did not mention on this questionnaire; we imagine that there are instances of both. As a step toward constructing a shared reality about practice, this therefore differs greatly from a more detailed and structured approach which would produce an accounting of, for example, the percentage of clinicians engaging in a specific practice or the entire range of types of practice in a particular category. Such an accounting may be a useful direction for future research.

Historically, political analysis has examined systems, groups and structures from an ideological base. This has resulted in a clear discussion of allocation of resources (e.g., wealth, decision-making power, public authority), but has neglected the personal and psychic impact on individuals. Most of psychology, alternatively, has focused primarily on the individual, to the exclusion of sociopolitical factors. Feminist therapy attempts to stand in both worlds, working from the double perspectives of the political and the psychological.

Politics looks different from inside the practice of therapy than it does from outside. The academic world, for example, which is the origin of much of the literature on therapy, looks at how power gets wielded in terms of status, the distribution and publication of theories, changes in the psychology of women over time, and theoretical analyses of issues. This perspective, while valuable, is not conducive to an examination of power as it is used personally and in relationship. Therapists, as the responses to this survey clearly show, think and talk about the implications of power in a real-world way. They reflect on their own use of power, how to offer power to others, and the implications in terms of power for a wide range of situations and behavior. Therapists look at how power is expressed in the context of clients' consciousness, lives and relationships. They do this daily and in a sophisticated and nuanced way. Feminist therapy thus becomes itself a form of action toward social change.

One's location in the standpoint of doing therapy changes how the issue of power looks and what one understands about it. Both this inside vantage point and the perspective available from outside of therapy are needed, but the internal standpoint has been less available in the literature to date. Political work gets reasoned and enacted in a very different way in the context of therapy, but it is political work nonetheless, giving lie to the claims sometimes made that feminist therapy practice has lost its political focus. Gail Anderson, in her survey response, said that "feminist therapy is radical and pervasive." What comes through most clearly in the comments of this group of experienced feminist therapists is a passion and clarity about a political stance which informs every detail of their work, from intake forms to relational nuances to modification of techniques. Feminist therapy thus becomes a lived experience of politics.

REFERENCES

American Psychological Association. (1992). *Ethical principles of psychologists and code of conduct*. Washington, DC: Author.

American Psychological Association (Producer). (1994). *Feminist therapy* [video]. In APA psychotherapy videotape series 1: Systems of psychotherapy. Washington, DC: Author.

Ballou, M. (1990). Approaching a feminist-principled paradigm in the construction of personality theory. In L.S. Brown & M.P. Root (Eds.), *Diversity and complexity in feminist therapy* (pp. 23-40). New York: The Haworth Press, Inc.

Ballou, M. (1995). Naming the issue. In E.J. Rave & C.C. Larsen (Eds.), *Ethical decision-making in therapy: Feminist perspectives* (pp. 42-56). New York: Guilford.

Ballou, M. & Gabalac, N. (1985). *A feminist position on mental health*. Springfield, IL: Charles Thomas.

Brodsky, A. (1980). A decade of feminist influence on psychotherapy. *Psychology of Women Quarterly*, 4, 331-344.

Brown, L. (1990). The meaning of a multicultural perspective for theory-building in feminist therapy. In L. Brown & M. Root (Eds.), *Diversity and complexity in feminist therapy* (pp. 1-21). New York: The Haworth Press, Inc.

Brown, L.S. (1994). *Subversive dialogues: Theory in feminist therapy*. New York: Basic Books.

Brown, L. & Ballou, M. (Eds.). (1992). *Personality and psychopathology: Feminist reappraisals*. New York: Guilford.

Brown, L. & Brodsky, A. (1992). The future of feminist therapy. *Psychotherapy*, *29*(1), 51-57.

Comas-Diaz, L. (1987). Feminist therapy and Hispanic/Latina women. *Women & Therapy*, *6*(4), 39-62.

Comas-Diaz, L. (1991). Feminism and diversity in psychology: The case of women of color. *Psychology of Women Quarterly*, *15*, 597-609.

Enns, C. (1992). Toward integrating feminist psychotherapy and feminist philosophy. *Professional Psychology: Research and Practice*, *23*, (6), 453-466.

Enns, C. (1993). Twenty years of feminist counseling and therapy: From naming biases to implementing multifaceted practice. *The Counseling Psychologist*, *21*(1), 3-87.

Espin, O. (1994). Feminist approaches. In L. Comas-Diaz & B. Greene (Eds.), *Women of color: Integrating ethnic and gender identities in psychotherapy* (pp. 265-286). New York: Guilford.

Espin, O. & Gawelek, M. (1992). Women's diversity: Ethnicity, race, class and gender in theories of feminist psychology. In L. Brown & M. Ballou (Eds.), *Personality and psychopathology: Feminist reappraisals*. New York: Guilford.

Feminist Therapy Institute. (1990). Feminist therapy code of ethics. In H. Lerman & M. Porter (Eds.), *Feminist ethics in psychotherapy* (pp. 37-40). New York: Springer.

Frye, M. (1983). *The politics of reality: Essays in feminist theory*. Trumansburg, NY: The Crossing Press.

Gilbert, L. (1980). Feminist therapy. In A. Brodsky & R. Hare-Mustin (Eds.), *Women and psychotherapy* (pp. 245-262). New York: Guilford.

Greenspan, M. (1983). *A new approach to women and therapy*. New York: McGraw-Hill.

Hammond, V.W. (1987). Conscious subjectivity or use of one's self in therapeutic process. *Women & Therapy*, *6*(4), 75-82.

Henwood, K. & Pidgen, N. (1995). Remaking the link: Research and standpoint theory. *Feminism and Psychology*, *5*(1), 7-30.

Hill, M. (1990). On creating a theory of feminist therapy. In L.S. Brown & M.P. Root (Eds.), *Diversity and complexity in feminist therapy* (pp. 53-66). New York: The Haworth Press, Inc.

Hill, M. (1992). A feminist model for paradoxical techniques in psychotherapy. *Professional Psychology: Research and Practice, 23*(4), 287-292.

Jordan, J., Kaplan, A., Miller, J.B., Stiver, I. & Surrey, J. (1991). *Women's growth in connection.* New York: Guilford.

Kanuha, V. (1990). The need for an integrated analysis of oppression in feminist therapy ethics. In H. Lerman & N. Porter (Eds.), *Feminist ethics in psychotherapy* (pp. 24-36). New York: Springer.

Kaschak, E. (1981). Feminist psychotherapy: The first decade. In S. Cox (Ed.), *Female psychology; The emerging self* (pp. 387-401). New York: St. Martin's Press.

Kaschak, E. (1992). *Engendered lives: A new psychology of women's experience.* New York: Basic Books.

Lerman, H. (1986). *A mote in Freud's eye: From psychoanalysis to psychology of women.* New York: Springer.

Leupnitz, D.A. (1988). *The family interpreted.* New York: Basic Books.

Rave, E.J. & Larsen, C.C. (Eds.). (1995). *Ethical decision-making in therapy; Feminist perspectives.* New York: Guilford.

Rawlings, E.I. & Carter, D.K. (1977). *Psychotherapy for women: Treatment toward equality.* Springfield, IL: Charles C Thomas.

Rosewater, L.B. & Walker, L. (Eds.). (1985). *Handbook of feminist therapy; Women's issues in psychotherapy.* New York: Springer.

Rothblum, E. & Cole, E. (Eds.). (1986). *A woman's recovery from the trauma of war.* New York: The Haworth Press, Inc.

Turner, C. (1991). Feminist practice with women of color: A developmental perspective. In M. Bricker-Jenkins, N.R. Hooyman & N. Gottlieb (Eds.), *Feminist social work practice in clinical settings* (pp. 108-127). Newbury Park, CA: Sage.

Webster, D. (1995, November). Adapting feminist therapy to managed care in the nineties. Paper presented at the Fourteenth Advanced Feminist Therapy Institute, Albuquerque, NM.

Whalen, M. (1996). *Counseling to end violence against women; A subversive model.* Newbury Park, CA: Sage.

White, M. & Epston, D. (1990). *Narrative means to therapeutic ends.* New York: William Norton.

Williams, E.F. (1976). *Notes of a feminist therapist.* New York: Dell.

Worell, J. & Remer, P. (1992). *Feminist perspectives in therapy: An empowerment model for women.* New York: Wiley.

Putting Politics into Practice:
Feminist Therapy as Feminist Praxis

Jeanne Marecek
Diane Kravetz

SUMMARY. A distinctive feature of feminist therapy is its insistence on bringing power into discussions of therapy and mental health. Using the framework of discourse analysis, we ask how feminist therapists talk about power. What linguistic resources do they employ to construct accounts of power in therapy? Drawing on interviews with three experienced feminist therapists, we trace how their language practices highlight some dimensions of power and conceal others. The diversity in these interviews points to the heterogeneity of feminist therapies. Although some feminist therapists are now calling for standardization, we argue that the field will be better served if diverse ideas and discourses are brought into abrasive interaction. *[Article copies available for a fee from The Haworth Document Delivery Service: 1-800-342-9678. E-mail address: getinfo@ haworth.com]*

Jeanne Marecek, PhD, is Professor of Psychology and head of Women's Studies at Swarthmore College. Diane Kravetz is Professor of Social Work at the University of Wisconsin-Madison. She has served as Director of the School of Social Work and chair of Women's Studies.

This article was written while Jeanne Marecek was a Fellow at the Swedish Collegium for Advanced Study in the Social Sciences in Uppsala; she gratefully acknowledges SCASSS's support.

Address correspondence to: Jeanne Marecek, Department of Psychology, Swarthmore College, 500 College Avenue, Swarthmore, PA 19081-1397.

[Haworth co-indexing entry note]: "Putting Politics into Practice: Feminist Therapy as Feminist Praxis." Marecek, Jeanne, and Diane Kravetz. Co-published simultaneously in *Women & Therapy* (The Haworth Press, Inc.) Vol. 21, No. 2, 1998, pp. 17-36; and: *Feminist Therapy as a Political Act* (ed: Marcia Hill) The Haworth Press, Inc., 1998, pp. 17-36; and: *Feminist Therapy as a Political Act* (ed: Marcia Hill) The Harrington Park Press, an imprint of The Haworth Press, Inc., 1998, pp. 17-36. Single or multiple copies of this article are available for a fee from The Haworth Document Delivery Service [1-800-342-9678, 9:00 a.m. - 5:00 p.m. (EST). E-mail address: getinfo@haworth.com].

© 1998 by The Haworth Press, Inc. All rights reserved.

Feminist therapy was conceived in the early 1970s in the oppositional spirit of the Women's Liberation Movement. Now, nearly 30 years later, feminist therapy—like feminism itself—has grown into a welter of approaches, ideas, politics, and practices (cf. Enns, 1997). One remnant of its original anti-establishment flavor persists: Feminist therapy remains for the most part outside the academy, its voluminous writings mostly outside the canon of the mental health professions (Brown, 1994; Marecek, 1993). Marginality has some advantages, as Laura Brown (1994) has pointed out. But it has drawbacks as well. One is the scarcity of systematic examination and exploration—even simple descriptive studies—of feminist therapy process or outcome, and of feminist therapists themselves.

In her call for papers, Marcia Hill, the editor of this volume, reminded us that "[f]eminist therapy by definition includes a political consciousness." "But," she went on to ask, "how is it that feminists politicize their work?" Working within a social constructionist framework, we pose her question in a slightly revised form: In their narratives about their work, how do feminist therapists address its political dimensions? What are the categories and terms by which power enters therapists' talk about therapy? In short, how do feminist therapists politicize (and perhaps on occasion depoliticize) their work through their language practices?

Neither institutionalized psychology nor psychiatry—the primary knowledge bases for most psychotherapy practice—has developed a language for talking about power. Indeed, both have been woefully reluctant to theorize how societal, institutional, or even interpersonal power differences might be connected to psychological distress and disorder (Kitzinger & Perkins, 1993). From the beginning, however, feminists have insisted on bringing power into discussions of therapy and mental health (e.g., Chesler, 1972). Without a hegemonic theory constraining them, feminist therapists have been able to draw upon many disparate concepts and language practices to theorize power.

For social constructionists, language practices create the objects of which we talk. Language is not a vehicle for expressing private and unique thoughts formulated inside a speaker's head; it is a social practice. As Potter (1996) says, "the terms and forms by which we achieve an understanding of the world and ourselves are . . . products of historically and culturally situated interchanges among people." These terms and forms—variously called discourses, interpretative repertoires, or consensual discursive practices—are systems of statements that cohere around meanings and values so habitual and familiar that they neither draw attention to themselves nor seem to demand analysis. They serve as rhetorical resources that enable speakers to construct accounts of themselves and the world that are intelligible and meaningful to listeners.

In this paper, we explore the interviews of three experienced feminist therapists drawn from a large set of interviews we have collected. The interviews serve as an arena where we can identify and explore some language practices of feminist therapists and also get at some of the meanings they generate. The therapists whose interviews we chose are typical of the larger group: they are white and middle class; their therapeutic approach is eclectic, drawing on a wide range of techniques and orientations. They are relatively experienced: each has at least 14 years of psychotherapy practice. We do not claim that these therapists are statistically representative of feminist therapists in general. Nor do we want to argue that three interviews exemplify specific categories of feminists or schools of feminist therapy. Our focus is on shared language practices and intersubjective meanings, not individual people. We seek to examine some discourses and terms available to feminist therapists for constructing accounts of their work. Analyzing the accounts further, we examine how these language practices highlight some meanings of power while concealing others.

METHOD

The interviews were conducted in the spring and summer of 1996 as part of a larger study. The interviewers were social work graduate students participating in a course on qualitative research methods. To recruit participants, feminist therapists who were known to the authors or the interviewers were contacted to request their participation and to generate the names of other therapists who might qualify for the study. Potential participants were contacted by telephone. This contact served both as an invitation to take part in the study and a screening interview to determine if the therapist was eligible. In the screening interview, we asked potential participants if they considered themselves to be feminists and if they brought a feminist perspective to their practice of therapy/counseling. We let potential participants define feminism for themselves; as Reinharz (1992) pointed out, feminism takes so many forms that it is impossible to impose a single universal definition on it. Therapy, too, takes so many forms that it is impossible to impose a single definition on it. Individuals who were in active practice of therapy or counseling and held an advanced (that is, post-baccalaureate) degree in one of the mental health specialties were included.

The interviews were carried out by advanced graduate students as part of a class on qualitative research in social work. The interviews lasted between one-and-a-half and two hours and consisted of broad, open-ended questions about feminism in therapy, with many probes for specific examples. All interviews were audiotaped and transcribed verbatim. We punctuated and paragraphed the transcripts, using our best judgment as to the intended meaning. Many of the therapists' narratives were informal and rambling, with sentence fragments, false starts, and digressions. The extracts presented below are not verbatim transcriptions; in the interests of brevity and ease of reading, we have edited out some dysfluencies and digressions.

Discourse analysis is the label for a set of approaches to working with texts and language, not a single formulaic research method. What discourse analytic approaches have in common is their attention to language and to the way that meanings are constructed. Discourse analysis is different from customary academic reading practices, in which one reads quickly for the "gist" of a passage. A discourse analyst attends to details of the talk or text, to the process—the twists and turns of language—by which it gets to its point. Clinicians who work in interpretive modes of therapy may see a resemblance to therapeutic listening processes. We agree that the mode of listening (or reading) is similar but there is a key difference. In a discourse analysis, the goal is not to infer mental states, defensive operations, inner thoughts, and the like. Instead we seek to identify the repertory of concepts and categories, and the systems of ideas, that the speakers, as competent members of the culture, rely on to create a narrative that is meaningful to listeners. And further, what does the use of this repertory achieve? What meanings *are* created? What tensions smoothed over? What paradoxes or contradictions seemingly resolved?

RESULTS: ANALYZING THERAPISTS' TALK

Therapist A: A Feminist Perspective Is a Healthy Perspective

A. opens her interview with a direct double reference to power (Table 1). To do feminist therapy is both to recognize women's lack of social, cultural, and political power and to work on empowering women in the therapy relationship (lines 2-7). Asked for specific examples of her therapy, A. shifts to a third theme: her concern about the power therapists have. The two anecdotes that A. narrates both concern times when she carefully and self-consciously restrained herself from imposing feminist goals and views on clients. ("You know," she says, "whether or not they would be *my* goals as a feminist, if those are *their* goals and they are mutually agreeable, then I know that I can't impose on those views.")

The link between abuse of power and imposing feminist goals on

TABLE 1

1 [I: What does it mean to you to say that your therapy is feminist?]
2 What does it mean to me? I think my view of it is, a cultural and political
3 one. That women do not as yet still have equal power in our society.
4 And so that when I'm working as a therapist, I work a lot on empowering
5 women and also recognizing the cultural and political overlays that make
6 that difficult and bring that into the personal context of whatever struggles
7 a particular client is having. And that my overall viewpoint is that it's
8 important to acknowledge the extent to which our culture is unhealthy in
9 terms of the goals that women have for themselves, the possible avenues to
10 being healthy. [. . .] I had a woman come in, in her late thirties, who's been
11 in a fourteen-year abusive marriage, and not left the marriage. And she
12 has one child, a son who's now 11 years old, who has begun to treat her
13 disrespectfully, and even be physical with her, and, that has been very-,
14 caused her to feel quite grief stricken at this change in the relationship.
15 [. . .] My overall perspective in what I'm saying to her is I can't help you
16 figure out how to keep a healthy relationship with your son while he has
17 this model . . . of you being treated abusively and disrespectfully by his
18 father.
19 [I: Do your feminist values conflict with your training as a therapist?]
20 [. . .] I don't think it's any more a conflict than the whole culture is in a
21 conflict toward feminism until it reaches that point where it is healthy,
22 which won't be in my lifetime. I guess it doesn't come up as much of a
23 conflict very often because I find that although people react very
24 negatively to the word feminist, I find that when you're working with
25 people to be healthy, if you can get the defense mechanisms out of the
way,
26 I don't think there's that much conflict about what changes may need to be
27 made. [. . .] I also have a lot of respect and, a sense of caution about the
28 amount of power I have as a therapist, and I'm very careful about that.
29 Right, because sometimes, I, sometimes, it's hard for me to think about
30 myself in that way because I have a very-. I think of myself as joining
31 with a person and working-. We're kind of a team and I have some skills.

TABLE 1 (continued)

32 But that each person has the answers and together we will discover them.
33 I don't have the answers, so in that context-. And that's how I think of
34 myself as I work. It is important that I remind myself that I, that
35 someone in the role of a therapist has a lot of power and you need to keep
36 that in mind so that you're very careful and respectful as you're working.
37 [I: Have there been times in therapy when you didn't act in accord with
38 your feminist principles?]
39 Hmm. (Long pause) I was trying to think what-. I mean, I work a lot with
40 women. In that context, I guess only in the ways that I had to accept what,
41 what is progress or success for someone in therapy might not be ideally
42 what I would like to see, but just a beginning in a certain direction. And
43 that's enough for that person for now and my feminist stuff might still-.
44 Well, injustice, or what I don't think is OK, or maybe the over-
45 accommodation of that female. Again, that's where as a feminist therapist,
46 and even as a therapist, you learn-. [. . .] It's important for me not to see
47 things as therapy failures which may be steps that people are taking or at
48 least having been heard in a certain way. Sometimes, you know, my wishes
49 for a client or my imaginings of where they are may not be correct. But
50 more can continue to happen after that person leaves therapy. And having
51 some things affirmed, therapy situation can create change that will be an
52 unfolding kind of change. And also sometimes that person will return. [. . .]
53 I'm not thinking of any direct conflicts. Although I am in some ways very
54 convinced of my perspective as healthy for men, women, and children in
55 our culture, I suppose there could be times in family therapy or in group
56 when I am waiting for the group or someone in the family to challenge
57 someone. And so it might not happen, and I have to work around to how
58 that's going to happen. It's not always my job to be taking on that role, but
59 to help the family speak together and, through highlighting and
60 emphasizing certain things, to have issues emerge and people willing to
61 speak up for the healthy viewpoints. So I suppose that I might feel
62 frustrated that it's not happening, but it's not in-, I suppose if I were
63 giving a speech to the family or the group, I would say "Look. Don't you

64 see-?" But in my role as a therapist, to promote that as coming within the
65 family or the group, it's not my job to prematurely serve that up to people.
66 Because it doesn't end up in change, and therefore just probably engenders
67 resistance. Being patient, and looking for opportunities to support the
68 more oppressed viewpoint–that would be the healthy viewpoint in the
69 situation–it's part of my job. I don't see that as a conflict.
70 [I: Do you identify yourself as a feminist therapist?]
71 I don't think I ever do. I feel that-, I mean that we all have our framework
72 and perspective and my job is to figure out how to work with someone in a
73 way that creates change for being a healthier person, and struggling less
74 in life, and being more satisfied in life. And I don't need to put a particular
75 label on that. I can't imagine-, I guess the point I'm at is-, I can't imagine
76 that anyone could be an effective healthy therapist without being a
77 feminist therapist. I mean, I just don't understand any way that it would be
78 incompatible with being a good therapist. But then I have my own
79 definition of who's a good therapist.

clients occurs again shortly (lines 27-36). This portion of the narrative
expresses a profusion of ideas about the power of therapists, as well as
evident discomfort with it. In the background is the tacit presumption that
therapists have a lot of power, creating a potentially dangerous situation.
A. takes pains to be respectful, cautious, and careful about this power
(lines 27-28). The next several sentences (lines 29-34), however, work
toward denying that A. has any power at all. She is merely part of a joint
effort, contributing only the skills to help clients discover the answers they
already have. The final sentence (lines 34-36), with its interplay of subject
pronouns (I, someone, you), affirms both the idea that "someone who is a
therapist" (not herself?) has power and that "you" (again, not herself?)
must be very careful and respectful. The concern about power is under-
scored by the link drawn between power and disrespect. A.'s initial use of
the term disrespect, in reference to an abusive father and son, placed it side
by side with physical abuse (lines 10-18).

An important theme in the narrative is that imposing (feminist) goals
and beliefs on clients is an abuse of power (e.g., lines 27-28 and 40-43).
Another, somewhat contrary, theme also figures importantly throughout
the narrative: that a feminist analysis of gendered power relations and
feminist-inspired goals are crucial for good therapy (e.g., lines 2-10;

20-26; 53-55; 75-77). But can a therapist engage in feminist-inspired analyses of clients' life situations and feminist-inspired solutions without "imposing" a point of view? How does the narrative construct a version of reality in which these two themes seem compatible? What strategies or language practices serve to dissolve or mask the tensions between them?

One language practice, the more prominent one, is what we shall call the health discourse. The words health and healthy occur twenty-three times in the course of the interview (e.g., lines 8-10; 15-17; 20-22; 24-27; 53-55; 71-73; 75-77). The term health is a powerful and popular rhetorical resource in modern western culture, one to which psychotherapists often have recourse. By "medicalizing" emotional distress and interpersonal troubles, the health discourse implies universal and objective norms and standards, not personal ideology. Moreover, it lends scientific authority and credibility to the ambiguities and moral complexities that surround emotional life, mental health, and psychotherapy. In A.'s narrative, the health discourse helps to dispel the dilemma of how to practice as a feminist without imposing feminist values and goals on clients. If feminist convictions and courses of action can be linguistically transformed into axioms of "good health," "healthy relationships," and even "effective healthy therapists," then one can have few qualms about imposing them on clients.

Another discourse also helps to manage tensions around feminist convictions: the idea of therapy as "a job" (e.g., lines 58-61; 64-65; 72-73). "It's just my job/It's not my job": Used in tandem, these phrases imply that therapy proceeds according to an objective and agreed-upon formula (akin to a job description); neither personal inclination nor feminist ideology governs how a therapist proceeds. The discourse of "doing my job" tends to routinize therapy practice, averting attention from the recognition that how A. defines and carries out therapy is shaped by her feminist politics.

At another level, we can ask how both the health discourse and the job discourse work to constitute the relationship between feminist practice and mainstream therapy. On the one hand, to assert that feminist principles are no more than universal principles of good mental health seems to challenge mainstream thinking. Yet, this assertion may ultimately be less transgressive than it first seems, because it stops short of challenging the apolitical and normalizing health discourse itself. As A.'s narrative ends, a note of harmonization with the mainstream prevails. The narrative closes with two rhetorical moves that close the gap between feminist therapy and the mainstream (lines 71-79). One negates any need to distinguish feminist therapy from the mainstream and the other denies feminist therapy a name.

Therapist B: Feminist Therapy as Pedagogy

B. specializes in domestic violence, working primarily with abusive men (Table 2). As can be seen in the excerpts, the interview coheres around a clear and consistent theme: Feminism is a commitment to stop men's oppression of women (lines 4-6). Feminism in therapy is educating men about abuse using methods of direct and relentless confrontation (lines 14-20). With men, B.'s mode of engagement is highly controlling, confrontational, and challenging (lines 24-25; 37-39; 55-58). Early in the narrative, B. momentarily notes a troubling paradox: that such a confrontative and controlling style verges on replicating the very behavior that it is intended to eliminate (lines 23-29). This fleeting recognition might have opened the way for further reflections on power dynamics in therapist-client relationships. It does not, however. Instead, the paradox is deflected by redescribing the issue as a matter of faulty technique and diminished effectiveness (lines 25-29).

Stepping back from that passage, we can ask the more general question of what rhetorical devices are deployed to take up issues of therapist-client power dynamics. The most evident one is the metaphor of therapy as teaching, a metaphor that is used repeatedly. Indeed, the terms teach, teaching, and educate occur over twenty times in the full transcript; they substitute for the term therapy, which is used only when B. is repeating the interviewer's question or referring to someone else's practice. Metaphors select and emphasize certain features of experience, while suppressing others; thus they impart meaning to that experience. When teaching is the dominant metaphor for therapy, what set of meanings are conveyed about the process of therapy and its goals? With regard to therapy process, the teaching metaphor works to cloak coercive actions on the part of a therapist with a mantle of acceptable benignity. As a teacher, a therapist is authorized to be didactic, confronting, and controlling. Indeed, the anecdote that vivifies B.'s approach suggests that merely the authoritative word of the therapist ("That's how you are abusive.") is sufficient to produce change (lines 14-20). The teaching metaphor also operates to sidestep issues of clients' autonomy and consent. Once therapy is figured as teaching, it may seem unproblematic for therapists to disregard clients' goals and impose their own without clients' knowledge or consent (lines 48-52).

The metaphor of therapy as teaching may also serve to legitimate feminist goals, to imply a cultural approval that such goals would not otherwise enjoy. Feminist ideas of equality in domestic relationships go against the grain of both the culture at large and the mental health professions. But teachers are, after all, culturally-sanctioned agents of socialization, and the

TABLE 2

1 [I: What does it mean to you to say that your therapy is feminist?]

2 So what does it mean to me to say that my therapy is feminist? . . . (T)hat I

3 really strive to focus on issues of equality, gender equality in the work that I

4 do. . . . (T)o say that I include feminism as part of my approach to therapy is

5 that I have a commitment to educate men about oppression, male oppression,

6 particularly of women. But just to look at all the ways men are socialized to

7 oppress other people, not just women, but across, you know, culture and

8 race. So it means that I have a commitment to educate men. It means that I

9 take a pretty active role in . . . confronting men about their oppression of

10 women. So what it means to me is it really, in every way or shape or form

11 that I do my work, I look for the differential in terms of equality. I look at

12 how people use privileged status, and so forth, and how that functions in

13 their lives, in their personal relationships, in the work world, and so forth.

14 And confront. [. . .] I'll say things like "It's real obvious that's the way you

15 have of controlling. OK, it's clear from your example, Jeff, that that's how

16 you are abusive. Real clear." . . . And the feminist part is to label that

17 behavior as a form of control. [. . .] And so he'll say things like "I'm trying

18 to get her to-." The minute he says "get her," that again is an example of

19 how he's becoming controlling . . . (A)nother piece of feminist theory is not

20 to let that slide.

21 [I: How have your ideas about feminist therapy changed over time?]

22 [. . .] I've gotten better in my ability to use that [feminism] in my therapy. I

23 think early on in therapy, I was probably much more blatantly

24 confrontive. You know, I just wanted to shake it out of these guys, kind of

25 thing. "What's the matter with you? Don't you get it?" Over the years, I've

26 learned how to get the message across in ways that are more effective. I

27 don't take them on so directly . . . And I think the end result is, is better.

28 'Cause I'm not modeling the very things that I'm trying to teach them not to

29 do.

30 [I: Have there been times when you felt that as a feminist you wanted to
act

31 in certain ways, but haven't?]

32 When I make errors, . . . it isn't because I have set aside my feminist ideology.

33 It's because I have been too strident in wanting to push the issue. [. . .] I

34 think, "I have to deal with this right now. This is such an egregious

35 breach of feminist ideology or equality." Or "this is too purely abusive" and

36 so on and so forth. [. . .] What I'm doing is not being subtle enough or not

37 being crafty enough. [. . .] I like to use the word (feminism) 'cause I like to

38 see how men react to it: "Feminism. Ugh. I don't want to be one of those

39 damn feminists."

40 [I: Are there clients . . . for which feminist therapy is especially helpful?]

41 Well, what do other people say?

42 [I: Well, some people have said domestic abuse. Or rape. You know, those

43 kinds of-, you know, the real societally, not even societally, serious

44 types of crimes.]

45 Oh God! Then they are missing how much abuse goes on.

46 [I: Are there individuals or types of problems you would not work with for

47 reasons connected to your feminism?]

48 There is probably no area I wouldn't want to. . . . No, in fact, even if somebody

49 came to me and said "I want you to help me be a better racist," for instance.

50 There are some people who-, you know, who have come in with some very

51 strange requests about therapy that I have really thought "Oh, wow! What

52 a great opportunity for me to teach somebody something here." [. . .] I

53 actually have more fun using feminism as a guiding principle in my work

54 with couples who aren't experiencing violence, and/or maybe with

55 violence. There is so much to confront. I have a lot more fun with couples

56 who come in because they can't communicate but there is not overt abuse.

57 . . . It's like "Well, I never considered that that was abusive." You know, it's

58 just fun to see them light up like a light bulb.

lessons they teach are culturally-authorized ones, the correct ways to be and behave.

In B.'s narrative, feminism itself can be seen as a rhetorical resource that is put to considerable use. B.'s allegiance to feminism is a source of self-assurance and confidence. As a feminist, B. can confidently dismiss mainstream training as wrong-headed: "Oh every bit of it! (Laughs) I've really had to work hard to overcome it." At the same time, B. is quick to take other feminist therapists to task for their shortcomings as feminists (lines 40-45). Yet the definition of feminism given in the narrative is a circumscribed, even idiosyncratic, one. For B., feminism is coterminous with ending individual men's abusive, controlling, and violent behavior toward individual women. The narrative reduces gendered power to the merely personal; the societal and institutional bases of gender inequality slide out of view. Moreover, the feminism in this narrative figures domestic violence in stark, black-and-white terms. Men are exclusively oppressors; women, hapless and helpless victims. The complex relational dynamics of couple abuse drop out of sight, along with women's subjectivity and agency. This version of feminism produces an image of a feminist therapist as a heroic figure who undertakes combat in order to rescue helpless women.

Therapist C.: My Religion Is My Kindness

C. introduces two themes that emerged in many other interviews, often intertwined as they are here (Table 3). One is women's connectedness or relationality, drawing in part on ideas of the Stone Center (Jordan, Kaplan, Miller, Stiver, & Surrey, 1992). The other is a congeries of ideas about spirituality, holistic health, and ecology associated with the New Age movement. C.'s ideas about therapy and mental health are framed within a dichotomy that is nearly totalizing: connection-disconnection. Connection is explicitly the province of women, the "ideas that women can bring" to a "starving" world; this, it seems, renders connection a "feminist principle" (lines 36-37; 57-60). Disconnection–by inference, the province of men–is both a metaphor for and a cause of human suffering, psychological disorders, and social malaise (lines 38-45). In the course of the narrative, an array of oppositions is aligned with that of disconnection-connection: conflict-collaboration, blaming-empathy, criticism-respect, discrimination-unity, anger-wisdom, human suffering-mental health.

For C., connection extends to a desire to dissolve differences and, at its outer limits, to an assertion of the unity of all matter, a cosmic oneness that is the dissolution of difference entirely. The narrative warrants the truth of connection by ascribing it not only to women, but also to an assortment of

TABLE 3

1 [I: What does it mean to you to say that your therapy is feminist?]

2 I think it means a consciousness of the relational model that is so important

3 to women and not blaming women for valuing that as they do, and the

4 choices they've made. Because of all the studies that have been done on

5 women's development. How they make decisions based on relationship.
And I

6 think it's easy to go in and blame women for that, rather than going in and

7 saying, "Well, that was a valuable thing." I think it means collaboration,

8 encouraging that, and valuing connectedness and empathy. And I think it

9 means respecting difference and not setting people apart, which I think

10 people in positions of less power have also been pitted. A real appreciation

11 for difference rather than-. [. . .] I do a lot of work with women around

12 issues in the workplace. [. . .] I will talk about the importance of having
your

13 intention clear, and having your, your goals clear, rather than operating

14 out of a model in which you would react-, you would be choosing your

15 actions from what your emotions and feelings and thoughts were. Which is

16 the way I think women get into trouble in terms of expressing themselves.

17 They either don't express it–for instance, when they get angry. And that

18 hap–, they either don't express themselves at all and stuff it, or they get

19 hysterical and lose the point. Not that that's always the case, but I think
that

20 that's often what happens, and then they don't get what they want. [. . .] So,

21 coaching them in a different way of being. At the same time, not judging

22 who they are. Not coming from a critical place. [. . .] I want to always
respect

23 people's boundaries, because so often when people come into therapy, I

24 mean, almost, I would say almost always, they have some issues with

25 boundaries, that their boundaries have been invaded in some ways. You

26 know, as women, and I think men, too. Women haven't known how to set

27 clearer limits for themselves. [. . .] I've been doing some more reading on

28 Native American stuff. And . . . I was reading about the mountains in Africa

TABLE 3 (continued)

29 and how prehistoric peoples believed that mountains were the petrified
30 form of their ancestors. Then when Christianity came in, it took a lot of
31 those things away. And what some people believe, which I think is very
32 interesting to think about, it would be real original disconnection came
33 with this whole mind-body thing, and our disconnection with the earth.
34 And now of course, all these, you know, people are making a lot of money
35 looking at this whole mind-body thing. Well, that's about connection, too.
36 So many of the things that are really coming into the forefront right now
37 are really based on feminist principles. Well, I think that they're about
38 connection. [. . .] You know, you think of when you work with people who
39 have an eating disorder or. . . . when people have addictions, I mean, the
40 ultimate is that you are so disconnected from yourself. . . . So, the
41 disconnection is on a personal level, but then it's on a family level, then it's
42 on a community level. It's really a larger political-. You know, people don't
43 feel connected to a lot of things in their lives. And it's really-. I was
44 reading this article by Judith Jordan. She was saying it's at the heart of
45 most human suffering.
46 [I: How have your ideas about feminist therapy changed over time?]
47 [. . .] And wisdom which comes with age, which is nice, you know. Because
48 you don't have to be so angry. [. . .] Well ideally, feminist therapy should be
49 about "Well, no, everybody doesn't have to think the same way." [. . .] I think
50 I have more, now, respect for people's right to feel differently. I've done a
51 Lot of work with conflict resolution. And specialized training in it and stuff,
52 and I do a lot of work with that. And to me, the ideas behind that are really
53 (chuckles) feminist, which is interesting. In the sense of working together,
54 and the idea of working in the circle, you know. People coming together to
55 stop to address problems and come up with solutions, and so. It's not about us
56 and them, but we're all together. We're all, you know, thinking about-.
57 We're all in this together. I think the world is starving for those kind of
58 ideas. The ideas that women can bring, that are, I think, grounded in

59 feminist principles in terms of collaboration and working together, and the
60 feeling of community, and-. [. . .] A client who I had seen for a year was
61 going through a divorce. Her son was getting married. And he was not
62 talking to her . . . And she was going to the wedding. And it was very
63 traumatic. She was going to go to this wedding. And I lent her this
64 rhinestone jewelry I have. Now some people think that was a really
65 inappropriate boundary of a therapist and a client. I am very clear
66 about my boundaries. [. . .] I really care about the people I work with. And I
67 told that to a friend who thought that it was terrible that I did that. So. You
68 know. I just think you have to trust yourself. I know there are a lot of
69 people out there practicing therapy that have poor boundaries. . . . I'm not
70 one of those people, you know.
71 [I: Are there other important issues . . . ?]
72 Well, it's the whole issue of how does it-, does it have to be set apart from
73 other therapy? I don't know. Is that important to have that as a definition?
74 I mean, I think I work that way, but it's not like I go around saying "I'm
75 a feminist therapist." That's not the label that I-, though it *is* a label. And I-.
76 Do you need the label? I don't know. Can you practice those things without
77 having a label attached to them? I would guess that some people think
78 there's power in the labeling. [. . .] I think I said to you, I don't necessarily
79 [label myself as a feminist therapist], and I certainly-. And it [the interview
80 protocol] says, "Why or how do you make these choices?" I make the choices
81 on-, this isn't about me; this is about the other person. [. . .] And there are
82 times when I choose not to identify myself, and I think that, sometimes, on
83 what, why and what conditions do I make this choice? I think it's like, if
84 somebody already feels really disempowered, I don't have to-, you know, you
85 know. I can show through actions, rather than identify-. Identifying
86 myself is again about me, not about them. It's kind of like the Dalai Lama's
87 quote, "My religion is my kindness."

exoticized peoples–pre-Christian Africans, Native Americans, and Tibetan Buddhists (lines 27-37)–and later to what she calls "that whole quantum physics stuff" . . . "the scientific-." Pragmatically and concretely, the theme of dissolving boundaries and differences informs C.'s approach to conflict resolution. She works to rise above differences in order to find and articulate common ground (lines 50-60).

The discourse of womanly connectedness, care, kindness, and empathy emerged among feminist theorists in the United States in the early 1980s. In the intervening years, a wide variety of criticisms of this line of thought have emerged. One was that the meaning of gender as male-female difference obliterated other meanings, especially that of gender as the system of power relations between the men and women (e.g., Hare-Mustin & Marecek, 1990). We can bring this concern about subjugated meanings of gender to bear on C.'s narrative. Does the emphasis on women's "difference," that is, their care and connection, jostle aside considerations of power relations? There are two features of the narrative where this concern seems pertinent. The first is the recurring concern for respecting and honoring difference. C.'s opening remarks distinguish feminist therapy as a therapy that does not blame (lines 2-7). It is, furthermore, coaching "without judging," "not coming from a critical place" (lines 20-22), and respecting clients' rights to be different (lines 49-50). Moreover, feminism in therapy entails taking care not to "invade" the boundaries of clients, and helping women "set clearer limits" for themselves (lines 22-27).

Respecting the ways that others are different from ourselves, however, is antithetical to asserting the unity, sameness, and common interests of us all. Yet in the version of reality that the narrative constructs, the two are made to seem like a seamless whole. How does the narrative achieve this? Connection, we suggest, has become a portmanteau or counterword–a word that conflates so many meanings together that it loses specificity. The term connection encompasses care, respect, empathy, kindness, unity, collaboration, and community, concepts that refer to disparate states and actions. What makes these disparate constructs seem related is their alignment with femininity in the connectedness discourse. Absent that alignment, the distinctions between them would become more evident. Of course, this conflation of meanings is not unique to C.; if it were, the narrative would not make sense to us.

We can explore the operation of the connectedness discourse further. Lines 60-70 are excerpts from a lengthy story about loaning jewelry to a client. C. describes this as a transgression of therapist-client boundaries, one that goes against the norms of mainstream practice and even of her friends. As most readers will know, many feminist therapists have challenged conventional therapist-client boundaries, arguing that norms of distanced neutrality violate feminist principles of egalitarianism and empowerment. C., however, does not describe loaning the jewelry as an effort to empower her client or to diminish the hierarchy between herself and her client. Instead the loan was an expression of "really caring about" the client. In a discursive world in which caring, kindness, unity, and respect are indistinguishable (all instances of connectedness), actions motivated by the therapist's caring feelings cannot by definition be intrusive, transgressive, or counter-therapeutic. Taking this theme a step further, the narrative asserts the primacy of a therapist's feelings ("staying true to yourself"; "trusting yourself"). It is these, in the end, that furnish the best guide for one's actions, better than one's training, the advice of friends, or ethical norms (lines 66-68).

Finally, the tension between respecting difference and asserting sameness reemerges in C.'s discussion of feminist therapy as an institution. "Who is to decide," she asks, "what is the definition of feminist therapy?" Instead of a definition, she wishes for a dialogue among feminist therapists in which "people honor in each other the different forms that their feminism has taken." Hard upon this wish that the differences among feminists be respected, she poses two further questions that strain toward dissolving difference: " . . . does it [feminist therapy] have to be set off from other therapy?" "[D]o you need the label?" Her answer to these questions is no (lines 72-85).

CONCLUSION: BRINGING THE DISCOURSES TOGETHER

In any interpretive project, the subjectivities and interests of the interpreters shape their stance. We are feminists who work in academic settings, not feminist therapists. We have been feminists since the 1970s; we cannot help but feel some nostalgia for the simpler world that feminists inhabited in those days and for the revolutionary zeal that carried us forward. Furthermore, we, like most of the therapists we interviewed, are white and relatively privileged. Our reading of the interviews is but one of the multiple possible readings; other interpreters vested with other interests would offer additional ones.

We also can ask how our methods of data collection shaped the outcome. The accounts that the therapists gave no doubt partly reflected their sense of the audience. The student interviewers varied considerably in their knowledge of feminism and of therapy. In response, participants may have assumed a "teacherly" stance, taking pains to clarify their ideas and supply context. Furthermore, the interview questions were intellectually demanding, requiring therapists to reflect on and synthesize their experiences, not simply to report them. The interview questions reflected our research question: How does feminism enter into and transform the practice of therapy? That question necessarily constrained the way the therapists answered. They focused on their feminism and how it inflected their work as therapists, and not on their theoretical commitments. Moreover, we learned only incidentally about how practicing therapy reshaped therapists' feminist politics.

In an earlier analysis, we had observed that for most participants, the distinctively feminist element of therapy was the client-therapist relationship (Marecek & Kravetz, 1997). This was true for both A. and C. But the elements they highlighted as distinctive to feminist therapy were not the same. For A., feminism sensitized her to her own power as a therapist. In consequence, she worked actively to subvert her own power–by giving priority to clients' values and goals, by self-consciously restraining herself from imposing her ideas and values, and by rhetorically disavowing it. C., on the other hand, did not speak directly about the power of the therapist. Her feminist principles centered on putting into practice the qualities and ideals that she associated with womanhood: caring, kindness, collaboration.

Sedimented in both A.'s and B.'s accounts, as well as in many others we have read, is a tacit presumption that women are powerless. But power, even gendered power, is neither so monolithic nor so static. Because it is transactional, power is always in flux; it can be negated, exchanged, modified, and even reversed. A key issue in contemporary feminist theory has been to devise ways to call attention to women's oppression and its debilitating effects without losing sight of their agency. How can we acknowledge the multiple hierarchies of power that people are situated in, acknowledging that a woman with little power in one situation may exercise power, perhaps even oppressive power, in another situation? And how should feminist therapists position themselves vis-à-vis clients–men or women–whom they view as exercising too much power? This question is raised in a compelling way by the account provided by B., one of the few participants who work with abusers. Nearly all the participants in the larger study refused to work with sexually or physically abusive men. Most said either that they were incapable of the confrontational and combative stance that such work required or they disliked it. Thus, it seems that the approach that B. describes is widely understood by feminist therapists as the proper therapeutic stance toward abusive men.

What can we conclude about the political consciousness of feminist therapists? Many political concerns flow through the narratives and we will not offer a tidy synthesis. Our project was investigative and descriptive, not normative and prescriptive. For A., concern about the way power operates in the therapy process takes precedence. B. is driven by a determination to end men's abuse of women. In contrast, C.'s politics run to a utopian desire to transform human consciousness to perceive the unity of all being and to espouse womanly ideals. Despite the striking differences in the therapists' feminisms, there was one aspect of political consciousness they had in common. All three were attuned to the current antifeminist backlash. A. and C., like nearly all the therapists in the larger study, were reluctant to identify themselves as feminists in professional contexts. B. reveled in the provocative power of the term feminist, but that power was conditioned on feminism's discredited popular status. These observations raise important questions about how the current culture of antifeminism operates to police and contain feminist therapists' identities and practices.

In the eyes of some workers in the field, institutionalizing feminist therapy is the next necessary step. The Division of the Psychology of Women, for example, is debating whether to petition the American Psychological Association for Specialty Recognition for Feminist Psychological Practice (Remer, 1996). Such status would likely entail codification of principles and practices of feminist therapy, standards for training, and the like. Our findings suggest that uniform standards of feminist practice would be nearly impossible to achieve. Just as there is no single definition of feminism nor one kind of feminist, there is no single meaning of feminist therapy, but rather a multiplicity of ideas about principles, processes, and therapy goals. Moreover, we question whether striving for uniformity and standardization is the best course of action at this point. Instead, the development of feminist therapy may be better served by bringing the disparate ideas of its practitioners into abrasive interaction. Finally, we prize feminist therapy for its oppositional character and its potential for critique of the psychotherapeutic mainstream (cf. Schuman & Gonzalez, 1996). Official standing within the mental health establishment may serve the goal of increased legitimacy, but we worry that such acceptance will come at the price of muffling feminists' critiques.

REFERENCES

Brown, L. (1994). *Subversive dialogues: Theory in feminist therapy*. New York: Basic Books.
Chesler, P. (1972). *Women and madness*. New York: Doubleday.
Enns, C. Z. (1997). *Feminist theories and feminist psychotherapies: Origins, themes, and variations*. New York: The Haworth Press, Inc.

Hare-Mustin, R. T., and Marecek, J. (1990). *Making a difference: Psychology and the construction of gender.* New Haven, CT: Yale.

Jordan, J. V., Kaplan, A. G., Miller, J. B., Stiver, I. P., and Surrey, J. L. (1992). *Women's growth in connection.* New York: Guilford Publications.

Kitzinger, C., and Perkins, R. (1993). *Changing our minds.* New York: New York University Press.

Marecek, J. (1993). Disappearances, silences, and anxious rhetoric: Gender in abnormal psychology textbooks. *Theoretical and Philosophical Psychology, 13* (2), 114-123.

Marecek, J., and Kravetz, D. (1997). Power and agency in feminist therapy. In C. Heenan and I. B. Seu (Eds.) *Contemporary feminist psychotherapies: Reflections on theory and practice.* London: Sage.

Potter, J. (1996). Discourse analysis and constructionist approaches: Theoretical background. In J. T. E. Richardson (Ed.) *Handbook of qualitative research methods.* Leicester: BPS Books.

Reinharz, S. (1992). *Feminist methods in social research.* New York: Oxford Univ. Press.

Remer, P. (Fall, 1996). Should Division 35 petition for specialty recognition for feminist psychological practice? *Psychology of Women Newsletter,* 19-20.

Schuman, J., and Gonzalez, M. (1996). A meta-/multi-discursive reading of "False Memory Syndrome." *Feminism and Psychology, 6* (1), 7-29.

Feminist Therapy:
Integrating Political Analysis
in Counseling and Psychotherapy

Susan L. Morrow
Donna M. Hawxhurst

SUMMARY. During its first decade, feminist therapy was rich with political analysis. Although many feminist therapists have remained loyal to that original stance, professionalization of feminist therapy has led to a de-emphasis on feminist political analysis. This article redefines and reclaims empowerment from a feminist political perspective and proposes a framework for conducting political analysis in feminist psychotherapy. *[Article copies available for a fee from The Haworth Document Delivery Service: 1-800-342-9678. E-mail address: getinfo@haworth.com]*

Susan L. Morrow, PhD, is Assistant Professor of Counseling Psychology at the University of Utah. She is a feminist psychologist, therapist, and supervisor and conducts research on feminist therapy, trauma, lesbian/gay/bisexual career development, and academic climate for women and people of color. Donna M. Hawxhurst, PhD, is a staff consultant at the Women's Resource Center at the University of Utah. She has developed and now participates in implementing a field practicum for graduate students in feminist therapy.

The authors wish to express their appreciation to Dorothy Riddle, who conceptualized the original empowerment model on which this work is based.

Address correspondence to: Susan L. Morrow, University of Utah, Department of Educational Psychology, 1705 E. Campus Center Drive, Room 327, Salt Lake City, UT 84112-9255 (E-mail: morrow@gse.utah.edu).

[Haworth co-indexing entry note]: "Feminist Therapy: Integrating Political Analysis in Counseling and Psychotherapy." Morrow, Susan L., and Donna M. Hawxhurst. Co-published simultaneously in *Women & Therapy* (The Haworth Press, Inc.) Vol. 21, No. 2, 1998, pp. 37-50; and: *Feminist Therapy as a Political Act* (ed: Marcia Hill) The Haworth Press, Inc., 1998, pp. 37-50; and: *Feminist Therapy as a Political Act* (ed: Marcia Hill) The Harrington Park Press, an imprint of The Haworth Press, Inc., 1998, pp. 37-50. Single or multiple copies of this article are available for a fee from The Haworth Document Delivery Service [1-800-342-9678, 9:00 a.m. - 5:00 p.m. (EST). E-mail address: getinfo@haworth.com].

© 1998 by The Haworth Press, Inc. All rights reserved.

37

Feminist therapy emerged from the United States Women's Liberation Movement in the 1960s and '70s. Very early in that movement, Mander and Rush (1974) wrote their classic book, *Feminism as Therapy,* stressing principles that were to undergird much of the early development of feminist counseling and psychotherapeutic practice: the idea that the personal is political, the importance of feminist consciousness-raising, and a critique of conventional models of psychotherapy. In addition, they introduced a holistic model that stressed the importance of working with women in relation to their bodies. Enns (1993) described the evolution of feminist therapy over the first two decades. The first decade was characterized by a critical examination of mental-health services to women, feminist consciousness-raising groups as an alternative to psychotherapy, an activist and grassroots orientation to therapy for women, an emphasis on groups as opposed to individual psychotherapy, and assertiveness training.

During the second decade of the evolution of feminist therapy, the discipline became more self-reflective and self-defining. Feminist therapy became gradually more professionalized, and feminist approaches to personality and therapy were proposed. Feminist professional journals increased from one to five in the field. Conventional approaches to diagnosis and assessment were criticized and feminist approaches proposed. Feminist personality theories and research methods and the integration of feminism with other psychotherapeutic approaches were addressed. Feminist theory was applied to identity development, career counseling, and particular populations such as lesbians and women of color. During this period, individual psychotherapy held sway, and groups were emphasized less than during the first decade. Multiple perspectives on feminist therapy proliferated, and ethics became a central topic of consideration. Feminist therapy became less political and activist as its therapists and clients became temporally removed from the Women's Liberation Movement of the 1970s. Research and teaching in feminist therapy became salient with the increased professionalization of the discipline.

The 1990s have brought additional research, as well as an integrative focus that includes a multicultural perspective in feminist therapy (Brown, 1994). Brown, as well as Espín (1994), have articulated the centrality of a multicultural approach to feminist therapy. Research during this period has expanded somewhat, with a focus on perceptions by potential clients of feminist therapists; attitudes and behaviors of feminist therapists; and the application of feminist therapy to specific populations and problems, particularly violence. As in the preceding period, grassroots activism plays a more minor role, although activism within the professional arena is common (Morrow & Beardsley, 1997).

The increasing professionalization of feminist therapy has resulted in several phenomena that are problematic for the field. Pressures of third-party payors and managed care providers have forced feminist therapists into the dilemma of "bending" diagnostic categories in order to avoid pathologizing clients while still utilizing reimbursable diagnoses or, on the other hand, capitulating to clinical diagnostic categories (Morrow & Beardsley, 1997). The former situation may result in feminist therapists walking a thin line between advocacy and ethical practice, while the latter flies in the face of many earlier feminist criticisms of traditional diagnosis and may result in feminist therapists compromising their political analyses and critiques of diagnostic labeling in an effort to manage the contradictions that face them. Clearly, a return to feminist therapy principles and activism is essential if we are to retain the core underpinnings of feminist practice.

Another challenge to feminist therapists presents as a supervisory dilemma. As state psychologist, social-work, and professional mental-health-counselor licensing laws place increasing restrictions on supervisors of mental health practice, including making supervisors legally responsible for client care, feminist supervisors increasingly find themselves refusing to take on supervisees, thereby limiting opportunities for feminist therapy training (Morrow & Beardsley, 1997). This trend may effectively curtail one of the major sources of information about and experience in feminist practice for new clinicians. Given this possibility, resources for future and current practitioners about how to conduct feminist therapy is sorely needed.

All of these challenges may be confronted by feminist therapists as avenues to continue to effect change. However, efforts by feminist therapists to fit into the mainstream of psychotherapeutic practice and academic contexts rather than challenging dominant paradigms also lead to the danger of compromising those most radical core feminist principles that led to the conceptualization of feminist practice as well as contributing to monumental changes thus far in the larger field of psychotherapy.

Kitzinger and Perkins (1993) noted that much of the early language of the Women's Movement and feminist therapy has been coopted by the mainstream of psychology, including such concepts as power, liberation, choice, and empowerment. What began, in the minds of early feminists, as political constructs have been transformed into individualistic phenomena. Now, we have power if we behave assertively in the family or workplace; we are liberated if we dance or beat drums in the woods; we exercise choice by weighing the pros and cons of staying in an unhealthy relationship or getting out–a kind of cost-benefit analysis. It appears as if the collective power of women, our liberation from oppression, or our right to choose how our bodies, sexuality, and reproductive functions are used have lost their place in feminist therapeutic analysis. Kitzinger and Perkins noted, "Psychology has used three different strategies to infiltrate our vocabulary. It has coopted and redefined existing political words; it has invented new depoliticized terms of its own; and it has tried to ban words from our vocabulary" (p. 37). Indeed, by attempting to adopt a neutral stance, there is no good or bad, right or wrong, no "shoulds." But, continued Kitzinger and Perkins, "Whatever it pretends, psychology is never 'apolitical'. It always serves to obscure larger social and political issues (sexism, heterosexism, racism, classism), connecting them into individual pathologies by an insistent focus on the personal" (p. 6). Critical of psychology as a depoliticizing force, Kitzinger and Perkins have questioned whether or not feminist psychology is an oxymoron.

PRINCIPLES OF FEMINIST THERAPY: RECLAIMING OUR ROOTS

In this article, we approach the theory and practice of feminist therapy with our experiences as feminist activists, therapists, and trainers for over two decades. We have continually challenged ourselves and each other about the constant pressure on us, as professional counselors and psychologists, to adopt the perspectives of mainstream practice, especially in relation to our work with survivors of childhood trauma. Whether or not feminism and psychology will eventually be proven to be mutually exclusive, we operate in a field of practice that we hope can combine personal healing with political transformation. Part of this ongoing challenge is to repeatedly revisit the principles and tenets of both early feminism and early feminist therapy theory and practice. These principles include:

The personal is political. The individual experiences of dis-ease experienced by women have their roots in the powerlessness and oppression of women as a class. Betty Friedan (1963) wrote of "the problem that has no name," describing women's psychological distress as a consequence of women's unexamined roles in society. Depression and other forms of psychological distress are created primarily by societal, cultural, and political forces.

A critique of conventional systems of psychotherapy. One of the earliest feminist criticisms of psychotherapy was that it encouraged women to adjust to their prescribed roles. Chesler (1972) illuminated the power dynamics between women and their psychotherapists, pointing out the ways in which women's departure from accepted roles was seen as pathology.

Feminism is *therapy* (Mander & Rush, 1974). Women talking and working collectively through consciousness-raising groups, political action, and grassroots movements such as rape recovery work or the battered women's movement provide many of the benefits typically expected of psychotherapy. These benefits accrue without financial cost in the context of power-equal peer relationships.

A simple return to early feminist therapy principles is, however, insufficient for our purposes as effective agents of political transformation. Feminist therapy as it is currently defined and practiced also must include an awareness of changing constructions of gender as well as a commitment to a multicultural perspective, in addition to the many other components that have come to define feminist therapy through its evolution. In this article, then, we reclaim and redefine empowerment to embrace its feminist roots and the important political changes and consciousness that have taken place over the last two and one-half decades–a lofty goal, no doubt. We include as well aspects of individual and interpersonal power, but always imbedded in a sociopolitical analysis.

EMPOWERMENT:
FEMINIST POLITICAL ANALYSIS IN PSYCHOTHERAPY

An empowerment model for feminist therapy must incorporate social/political factors in women's lives. In this article, we define empowerment as a process of changing the internal and external conditions of people's lives, in the interests of social equity and justice, through individual and collective analysis and action that has as its catalyst a political analysis. In the conceptual framework that follows, we expand on and illustrate what we mean by empowerment in feminist therapy.

The framework for empowerment that we have developed and used in our practice and training over time acknowledges those personal and interpersonal aspects of power that have come to embody the concept of empowerment in recent years. We have reframed those aspects from a feminist perspective as well as added a sociopolitical aspect. This framework for empowerment is imbedded in the context of a feminist political analysis, and it is these feminist political origins that we especially wish to reclaim and reintegrate into the concept and process of feminist therapy. Dorothy Riddle was the author of our original framework for using political analysis in psychotherapy. Over the years, we have expanded her framework to its present form, which we see as a conceptual model, a process, and a tool for conducting political analysis in psychotherapy. In this section, we present and describe the framework, followed by its application to brief case examples. Our emphasis will be on feminist political analysis in therapy applied not only to the personal and interpersonal perspectives emphasized in current popular literature on personal growth and psychotherapy, but also the social/political structures and processes that either enhance or limit one's access to an empowered life.

An empowerment framework may be conceptualized as consisting of both dimensions of and conditions for empowerment. The dimensions of empowerment include personal, interpersonal, and social/political levels of power; and, at each of these levels, in order to become empowered, an individual must experience permission, enablement, and information. It should be noted here that the original word "enablement" was used in the model before it became part of the popular discourse related to substance abuse; as we have yet to identify a term that adequately depicts our meaning described below, we have chosen to keep the term here. The dimensions and conditions of empowerment are illustrated in Figure 1.

Dimensions of empowerment. The dimensions of empowerment are personal, interpersonal, and social/political. At the personal dimension, empowerment is concerned with the intrapersonal and intrapsychic aspects of an individual's experience, the traditional purview of conventional individual psychology and psychotherapy. However, this level is conceived of differently by feminist therapists than by conventional therapists, and, in fact, must include contextual and political analyses. The personal dimension focuses on power within the person and involves acknowledging, gaining, maintaining, or restoring power and control over an aspect of one's life. It assumes that an individual has access to some degree of personal power, energy, and ability to act in her or his own behalf, as well as the right and potential to exercise it. Empowerment at this level may include working through early traumatic events or reframing parental messages so that those who in fact did have power at one time to control, influence, or abuse no longer hold that power. It includes an analysis of the power dynamics related to those who formerly held overt power over an individual's life–parents, caretakers, older siblings, teachers, and others in positions of authority or privilege. Abuses by these individuals of their power and control may have become internalized by the child, continuing to influence and limit her or his possibilities long after the external controls are gone. Analysis of parental and other messages take on a feminist cast when addressed in the context of social/political norms, e.g., when a mother's injunctions to her daughter not to be too assertive are placed in perspective of the mother's female socialization. Of particular importance to feminist therapists is the concept of internalized oppression, in which misogyny, racism, classism, heterosexism, and other forms of prejudice or hatred are incorporated into an individual's own self-concept, effectively

FIGURE 1. Conditions and Dimensions of Empowerment in Feminist Therapy.

Dimensions of Empowerment

Conditions for Empowerment	Personal (Power within)	Interpersonal (Power with others)	Sociopolitical (Power in society)
Permission (May I? Am I worthy?)	Individual rights and freedoms	Approval or permission from another	Legal rights
Enablement (Can I? Am I able?)	Personal resources	Support and advocacy from others	Access to resources
Information (What do I need to know?)	"Know thyself"	Sharing stories, breaking silences	Questioning "the truth"

restricting the possibilities for empowerment at a personal level. At the personal dimension, the therapy goal might be to move from self-hatred and self-denial to self-love and nurturing, recognizing the strengths of inner resources and the often-improbable reality of one's survival in the face of seemingly impossible circumstances. Feminist reframing of "pathology" or "dysfunction" as positive coping strategies (Morrow & Smith, 1995) is a valuable tool in this process of empowerment. As the feminist therapist works with a client at this dimension of empowerment, there are often obstacles that must first be overcome before a process of personal empowerment can occur; these obstacles may present at the interpersonal (e.g., a current abusive relationship) or social/political dimension (e.g., poverty).

The interpersonal dimension represents the many experiences of power and powerlessness that occur at the interpersonal level or have an interpersonal overlay–that is, where others currently in the client's life, such as spouses, partners, friends, family, coworkers, and acquaintances, are able to enhance or limit her personal power. Often personal power issues become interpersonal power struggles or power failures, e.g., when a friend, partner, or therapist becomes invested in or takes responsibility for another's process or outcomes. Also at the interpersonal level are those who maintain power and control by virtue of their position of dominance, defined and maintained by such characteristics as gender, race, institutionalized authority, economic privilege, or other entitlements. For example, an abusive, violent spouse or partner can effectively block a woman's possibilities for recognizing her potential for personal power. Empowerment at an interpersonal level is based upon a necessity to address issues of power, dominance, and privilege in relationships, recognizing that, when hierarchy is unavoidable, the limits of equality are very real (e.g., in many traditional work settings and even intimate relationships). At the interpersonal level of empowerment, egalitarian relationships are valued and based on mutuality, consensual decision making, and collaboration. In relationships in which power imbalances are implicit or unavoidable, such as the therapy relationship, the more powerful individual–in this case the therapist–would strive to incorporate characteristics of an egalitarian relationship, making explicit the possibilities and limits of this endeavor. When hierarchy is unavoidable, interpersonal empowerment may be limited yet maximized by developing strategies for remaining empowered in so far as possible, depending upon opportunities for safety, support, collaboration, and feedback.

At the social/political dimension, there are limits and barriers imposed by social laws, norms, values, rules, sanctions, taboos, and prejudices that perpetuate injustices. When the social/political level is unacknowledged, an individual is likely to blame her/himself for life circumstances. It is often necessary to understand the nature of privilege and power relations in regard to, for example, gender, race, class, ethnicity, or sexual orientation in order to achieve empowerment at the personal or interpersonal dimensions. Access to resources in society is greatly influenced, if not dictated, by one's position in an elaborate hierarchy of membership in various reference groups. The historical roots of discrepancies in privilege and access are based upon the politics of domination and colonization, resulting in institutionalized systems of subordination and oppression that are presented to us as "reality." Social/political empowerment requires group support, action, and movement in order to ultimately move beyond or through the barriers imposed by the existing social/political structures and functions. Feminist counseling or therapy must include a political analysis of the broader sociopolitical context, as well as action, in order to be effective.

Empowerment consists of analyzing power and identifying potential action at the personal, interpersonal, and social dimensions. At each dimension are conditions–permission, enablement, and information–that must operate in order for empowerment to occur.

Conditions for empowerment. Conditions for empowerment include permission, enablement, and information, appearing in Figure 1 and presented here as discrete, separate categories. These conditions are clearly interrelated and interdependent and cannot be achieved without the others. Each condition–permission, enablement, and information–operates on all three dimensions–personal, interpersonal, and sociopolitical–of empowerment.

Permission involves addressing the questions, "May I?" "Do I have the right?" "What am I entitled to?" or even, "Am I worthy?" At the *personal dimension,* permission involves recognizing, knowing, naming, and believing that one deserves to have individual rights and freedoms, love, friendship, and the many things that create a high-quality life. At the *interpersonal dimension,* permission involves the real or perceived requirement of permission-giving by another. There may be severe consequences to acting in one's own behalf, for example, in a relationship in which power and control are maintained through violence or the threat of violence. On the other hand, an individual may perceive that s/he requires permission from another when that is not the case. It is important to consider the power and consequences of approval and disapproval by another as well as the more overt risks involving physical danger. Addressing questions of ownership, obligation, entitlement, and consequences is useful when considering permission at the interpersonal level. Permission at the *social/political dimension* involves examining laws, rules, norms, values, and prohibitions that either support or undermine a person's rights and freedoms. Some questions that may be relevant to this level include, "What are my legal rights?" "What are the consequences of violating legal or social prohibitions?" and "How is obedience enforced/reinforced?"

Enablement addresses the questions, "Can I?" and "How can I?" Again, this term does not imply codependence. In an empowerment framework, it relates to having or gaining abilities or other resources for empowerment. At the *personal dimension,* enablement involves identifying one's abilities, skills, knowledges, and other personal resources and determining ways to acquire or enhance these resources through education, training, employment, funding, therapy, or other means. At the *interpersonal dimension,* enablement involves mentoring, support, assistance, or facilitation within the context of individual or group relationships through such actions as networking, support or consciousness-raising groups, or individual advocacy for another person. At the *social/political dimension,* enablement involves the provision of and access to resources, opportunities, and freedoms. Action at this level would include the implementation and enforcement of affirmative action policies, civil rights laws, and stated values of equal opportunity, multiculturalism, and social justice.

Information addresses the questions, "What do I need to know?," "What are the questions I do not know to ask?" and "Where do I find the information I need?" At all levels information is power that can be used to either limit or expand one's possibilities. At the *personal dimension,* an individual would be concerned with information about herself–her interests, needs, priorities, history, identity, aptitudes, health, coping strategies, and a host of other personal characteristics. "Know thyself" best describes the condition of information at the personal level. At the *interpersonal dimension,* information is exchanged through women telling stories, giving voice to their experiences, sharing the secrets that have burdened them, and breaking the silences that have kept them imprisoned and isolated. In therapy, the therapist can provide information about resources and patriarchal lies as well as helping the client ask questions s/he has not considered. At the *social/political dimension,* information involves identifying and understanding the lenses through which information is presented via popular culture, professions, and educational and other social institutions. This process includes examining information *about* information, that is, institutionalized censorship (the withholding of information), as well as the selective presentation of information designed to maintain the status quo. Translating and critically analyzing information that is convincingly and authoritatively presented as "the truth" are critical aspects of understanding how information contributes to or limits empowerment at the social/political dimension. Of particular importance to feminist therapists and their clients is diagnostic information from the *Diagnostic and Statistical Manual of Mental Disorders* (DSM-IV, American Psychiatric Association, 1994), presented and often interpreted as conclusive, well-founded scientific data.

FEMINIST POLITICAL ANALYSIS AND ACTION: USING EMPOWERMENT PRINCIPLES IN THERAPY

Just as conventional psychotherapy depends on a number of components–awareness, cognitive strategies, and behavior change, to mention just three–to be effective, feminist therapy incorporates those strategies as well as two others: *analysis* and *action.* Awareness, by itself, may at times be a sufficient tool to enhance a client's growth and well-being in conventional psychotherapy; in the same way, analysis alone may help to frame a situation in a way that may be empowering in feminist therapy. However, action, like behavior change, may be necessary in order for empowerment to occur in many other circumstances. The framework illustrated in Figure 2, along with some examples from therapy sessions, may help to clarify ways in which a therapist may work in an empowering way. Cases are referred to in the figure by number in parenthesis.

Case 1 (C1): Childhood sexual-abuse survivor. Sarah is an African-American woman who has presented with symptoms (depression and inability to achieve orgasm during heterosexual sex) as well as partial memories of having been sexually abused by her stepfather. During early therapy sessions, client and therapist have addressed the conditions and dimensions of empowerment as they relate to her situation as well as mutually agreeing on appropriate action. They have discussed her doubts and concerns regarding her early abuse, which stem from messages from the perpetrator that no one would believe her if she told them she was being abused, as well as societal messages regarding "false memories." Addressing her sexual difficulties, Sarah discovers that she lacks information about female sexuality, is afraid her partner does not believe she was abused or will grow impatient with her, and experiences intermittent flashes of fear during sex that affect her desire. She also discovers that she wants to be fully sexual. Her partner believes her and wants to be supportive; he is willing to try exercises suggested by the therapist that maintain the client's control of sexual behaviors while she is working through effects of the abuse. The therapist provides verbal information and suggests readings to Sarah about recovered memories.

FIGURE 2. Incorporating Political Analysis in Feminist Therapy in Three Cases.

Dimensions of Empowerment

	Personal (Power within)	Interpersonal (Power with others)	Sociopolitical (Power in society)
Permission (May I? Am I worthy?)	C1-Internalized message that she will not be believed C3-Analysis of effects of battering on self-esteem	C1-Partner is supportive; therapist works for mutuality in decisions C3-Mentally reject assessments of violent partner with help of validation of therapist	C1-Analyze politics of repressed memories; normalize reactions to sexual abuse C2-Societal messages re: appropriate careers & roles for women
Enablement (Can I? Am I able?)	C2-Uncertain re: abilities due to nontraditional career + gender conflict; clarification of competence C3-Personal safety plan & action	C1-Exercise maintaining control of sexual behaviors C2-Analysis skills of gender roles in relationship & society	C3-Analysis of interplay of racism/homophobia to keep client powerless C3-Resources for safety, support, & healing
Information (What do I need to know?)	C1-Exploration of feelings about sex	C1-Education re: female sex response C3-Information re: battering, resources for safety, support, healing	C1-Recovered memory controversy & politics C3-Resources for battered women that are lesbian- & Latina-supportive

Conditions for Empowerment

Case 2 (C2): Career conflict. Shelly is a White pre-veterinary student at the university. She has wanted to be a vet since childhood, but as she approaches graduation, she has become less certain about her abilities and intelligence. As Shelly and her therapist explore her uncertainty, they discover that Shelly has a 3.9 grade-point average, has been at the top of her class throughout her pre-veterinary training, and is likely to receive scholarships to a number of veterinary schools. She also recently became serious about a young man, also preparing to be a veterinarian, whose top choice of schools differs from Shelly's. Because of their conflicts, Shelly is uncertain about how to prioritize her own career needs. Shelly and her boyfriend work together in therapy, addressing their own personal needs and strengths as well as societal messages about appropriate roles for men and women. The therapist assists the couple in expanding their communication skills to include an analysis of gendered dynamics in their relationship and in society.

Case 3 (C3): Partner abuse. Gloria, a Latina with two small children, is in relationship of one year with a Caucasian woman. She seeks counseling because of depression, which began about six months earlier. She appears fearful and indicates that her self-esteem is "in the basement." Over a period of several weeks of therapy, she finally acknowledges that her partner has been pushing and occasionally hitting her, as well as using racial slurs. The partner has also threatened that, if Gloria tries to leave her, she will inform Gloria's husband that Gloria is a lesbian. Gloria fears losing her children but is also concerned about the children being raised in a violent household. She blames herself for irritating her partner and has begun to question her ability to be a good mother. Her therapist helps her examine the impact of battering–including racist and homophobic abuse–on her self-esteem, shares information about battering dynamics, identifies safety as a primary concern, and helps Gloria find legal and battered women's resources that are both lesbian and Latina-affirmative.

These three cases, illustrated in Figure 2, provide suggestions for applying the empowerment framework to practice. Therapists will have different analyses of these situations, and the reader may find some areas of empowerment more relevant than others depending upon the context.

THE PAST AND FUTURE OF POLITICAL ANALYSIS AND ACTION IN PSYCHOTHERAPY

Feminist therapy has a rich past, particularly from its first decade, of political analysis and action. Many feminist therapists over the past decade have not had the benefit of involvement in the early Women's Liberation

Movement, while others have moved into a more professionalized arena as psychotherapists. Still others have embraced a transpersonal or spiritual dimension, sometimes to the exclusion of political analysis and action. However, a minority of feminist therapists have maintained their political roots, and current multicultural feminist authors from both practice and academe have brought political thought and analysis back to the forefront.

With over two-and-one-half decades of practice and research, feminist therapy is rich with theory. However, outside the training arena, little has been articulated about what feminist therapists do that distinguishes them from other therapeutic approaches. Feminist psychotherapy is in jeopardy from managed care, licensing regulations, and other forces unless it can define and, ultimately, demonstrate the effectiveness of, its techniques and strategies. This article offers a particular strategy for analysis and action that is unique to feminist therapy and can be used in practice as well as investigated further for its effectiveness as a psychotherapeutic tool. The integrity of feminist therapy depends both on its adherence to its political roots as well as the evolution of its theory and practice in the future.

REFERENCES

American Psychiatric Association. (1994). *Diagnostic and statistical manual of mental disorders* (4th ed.). Washington, DC: Author.

Brown, L. S. (1994). *Subversive dialogues: Theory in feminist therapy*. New York: Basic Books.

Chesler, P. (1972). *Women and madness*. New York: Doubleday.

Enns, C. Z. (1993). Twenty years of feminist counseling and therapy: From naming biases to implementing multifaceted practice. *The Counseling Psychologist, 21*, 3-87.

Espín, O. (1994). Feminist approaches. In L. Comas-Díaz & B. Greene (Eds.), *Women of color: Integrating ethnic and gender identities in psychotherapy* (pp. 265-286).

Friedan, B. (1963). *The feminine mystique*. New York: Dell.

Kitzinger, C., & Perkins, R. (1993). *Changing our minds: Lesbian feminism and psychology*. New York: New York University Press.

Mander, A. V., & Rush, A. K. (1974). *Feminism as therapy*. New York: Random House.

Morrow, S. L., & Beardsley, R. (1997). [Experiences and perceptions of experienced feminist therapists: A qualitative investigation.] Unpublished raw data.

Morrow, S. L., & Smith, M. L. (1995). Constructions of survival and coping by women who have survived childhood sexual abuse. *Journal of Counseling Psychology, 42*, 24-33.

Contextual Identity:
A Model for Therapy and Social Change

Susan E. Barrett

SUMMARY. Identity is a complex construct, involving the integration of multiple views of oneself. We are individuals, members of families and communities, part of larger social groupings, such as race and class, and also part of the universal family of humans. This paper focuses on the importance of integrating group identity, both from minority and dominant positions, into a personal understanding of oneself and one's connections. Particular topics include: integration of group identities with individual ones; communication between people with different group identities; and implications for social change efforts. *[Article copies available for a fee from The Haworth Document Delivery Service: 1-800-342-9678. E-mail address: getinfo@haworth.com]*

Questions and issues of self-identity underlie much of how we know ourselves and each other. All of us have a number of ways we describe who we are. As an individual, we are each unique, exhibiting a variety of personality patterns and interests that stay remarkably stable across time and allow us to differentiate ourselves from others. We are also embedded in a range of social contexts, including families, friends, and communities

Susan E. Barrett, PhD, is a psychologist in independent practice in Atlanta. Her ideas are filtered through her own identities as a white, middle-class, able-bodied lesbian in a bicultural, biracial family.

Address correspondence to: Susan E. Barrett, PhD, 1904 Monroe Drive, N.E., Suite 200, Atlanta, GA 30324.

[Haworth co-indexing entry note]: "Contextual Identity: A Model for Therapy and Social Change." Barrett, Susan E. Co-published simultaneously in *Women & Therapy* (The Haworth Press, Inc.) Vol. 21, No. 2, 1998, pp. 51-64; and: *Feminist Therapy as a Political Act* (ed: Marcia Hill) The Haworth Press, Inc., 1998, pp. 51-64; and: *Feminist Therapy as a Political Act* (ed: Marcia Hill) The Harrington Park Press, an imprint of The Haworth Press, Inc., 1998, pp. 51-64. Single or multiple copies of this article are available for a fee from The Haworth Document Delivery Service [1-800-342-9678, 9:00 a.m. - 5:00 p.m. (EST). E-mail address: getinfo@haworth.com].

© 1998 by The Haworth Press, Inc. All rights reserved.

51

which may vary across time resulting in different roles we play, e.g., moving from being a daughter to also being a mother. Beyond these personal levels of identity, we have a sense of self based on larger social units, such as race, class and country in which we live. Finally, we also have an identity that is more universal, transcending differences, based on being human.

As therapists, the aspects of identity on which we choose to focus frame how we view ourselves, our clients and our work. Consciousness around our choice of framework is one aspect of political activity, that of theory building. Theoretical understanding of identity in Western psychology has heavily emphasized the individuality of each person. Substantial groups of therapists go beyond the individual to include the relational aspects of identity, e.g., families and friends. As a profession, however, we have done less well integrating group identity, beyond the level of particular friends, with the individual identity. Instead, we have left the concept of group identity primarily to those interested in social change through "identity politics." And, though most of us might use a concept of the universal human in our therapeutic work, just what psychological characteristics we actually share with all others has been so heavily influenced by the thinking of those in dominant group positions that what is truly universal is far from clear.

A complex, contexual frame for understanding the identity of ourselves and others provides a much fuller, more integrated sense of self than an emphasis on any one or two of the various areas. Though at any given time an individual may focus on a particular form of identity, in general all levels need to be included in a full sense of self. This article focuses on the importance of group identity for individuals in therapy and in particular the integration of group identity, from both a minority and majority position, into a personal understanding of oneself and one's connections.

Many people have an integrated, contextual identity but may not have the language to describe it. Maria is such an example. She is a 51-year-old woman, born and raised in Puerto Rico and living in the United States since she was 25. She teaches at a university where she is well-respected as a teacher and as a supporter of women's rights. She has two adult children, is divorced and currently lives alone. She is bilingual and bicultural and has worked to instill both cultures in her children. She routinely experiences both the devaluing and valuing of herself based on her identities as a member of various groups. For example, she is heterosexual, well-educated, raised in upper class society in Puerto Rico, and has a prestigious job. She clearly benefits from falling into those groups and has developed personal styles of being, e.g., competent and proficient, that capitalize on the benefits. She also experiences loneliness and a lack of connection when trying to develop friendships with her colleagues/friends who do not have the same deep sense of family and openness to connection that she has. Her white, North American friends don't truly grasp her way of being with her children, for example. She addresses the pain and vulnerability that result from racism and emotional isolation by keeping strong connections to other women from a variety of non-white backgrounds. She struggles within herself with putting together her deep need for connection and her desire not to appear vulnerable. Mostly, she is able to experience herself as part of several worlds and to move comfortably among them (Lugones, 1990).

INTEGRATION OF POSITIVE MINORITY GROUP IDENTITY WITH INDIVIDUAL IDENTITY

Karen is a Chinese-American woman, born and raised in the United States. Her parents were born and raised in China, emigrating as adults. Although her parents maintained connections with Chinese friends and passed on to Karen some aspects of Chinese culture, she herself was raised completely within white communities and saw herself as white. Her father was instrumental in this, seeing himself as a businessman successful within white American culture. Karen had lived for a long time in Hawaii and the West Coast. It was only when she moved to the East Coast with an extremely small Asian community, that it become clear to her that she indeed is Chinese-American. Her adoption of a daughter born in China has clarified that understanding even more. She has made the decision to move back to the West Coast as an affirmation of her need to have her family more firmly embedded in Asian-American communities. Truly seeing herself as Chinese-American has given Karen a fuller sense of herself, a deeper grounding in the world, and an additional bond between herself and her daughter.

Many racial and ethnic minority individuals are raised with a strong positive identity based in that cultural heritage. Ethnic communities and cultural institutions such as churches, clubs and organizations can clearly provide a sense of pride in belonging to that particular group. Even when living without easy access to like-others, children can be raised with a positive minority group identity if efforts are made by the parents to provide an understanding of cultural identity and to make connections with others of that group. However, living within the dominant culture can make intimate connections across race and culture difficult (Tatum, 1993).

Other individuals and groups, however, are not raised to value themselves. A prime example is lesbian and gay youth who usually grow to adulthood with a strong internalization of the negative views of society toward homosexuals. Even people raised with strong positive minority group beliefs frequently have, at the same time, internalized negative views of themselves, absorbed through the multiple ways society devalues them (e.g., internalized racism). Janet Helms (1990) in her book on *Black and White Racial Identity* summarizes the work of some theorists on the development of a positive minority racial identity. These ideas have also been used to discuss identity development of other minorities, including lesbians and gay men (Barrett, 1990). In the models represented in this group, individuals move through a process that begins with an absorption of the negative images of society placed upon their group (internalized racism, internalized homophobia). A transition phase in which that identity is inconsistent with other aspects of one's identity (e.g., I am smart), leads to a turning toward like others and learning to value the positive parts of that identity (Black is beautiful, women loving other women is good). Here the primary focus is away from the dominant group and toward the minority group. At some point in time, this focus begins to feel limiting since all aspects of oneself are not addressed by virtue of that particular group and one moves to a more universal position, recognizing the commonalities among various minority groups. This transition of how to value oneself in a world that devalues you is critical to make for those in a dominated position (Adleman & Enguidanos, 1994).

With regard to an integrated sense of identity, minority individuals need to be able to separate reactions to them personally from reactions to them that are prejudices of the dominant group. For example, if a lesbian is ignored in a discussion, she needs to be able to tell if that is a reaction to her individually or if it is a homophobic reaction on the part of others. If an African-American woman is not asked to chair a committee, she needs to know whether that is racist behavior and/or a reaction to her individually. This ability to catagorize other people's behavior accurately is difficult at best, is very hard to do in isolation without feedback from others, and is often impossible because some behaviors are both, i.e., a response to an individual qua individual and a racist behavior at the same time. Promotions and firings are argued from these two positions constantly; "I was fired because she/he was racist." "I fired her/him because she/he didn't do the work." In many situations it is far from clear what is the prejudicial attitude toward another culture's view of time, for instance, and what is important behavior on the part of employees, e.g., to arrive at work promptly.

An inability to shift between group identity and individual identity can leave a minority individual at risk in one of two ways. First, she/he can personalize the prejudice that is coming toward her/him, believing it is she/he who is "not good" rather than that the other person is racist. Obviously, this is a personally difficult and demeaning position in which to be. If the individual is not connected to others in a way that allows her/him to check out the perception, the problem is compounded. On the other hand, individuals can minimize their personal responsibility for their lives if they attribute everything that happens as a response to their minority status. The person can often feel victimized and immobilized, stuck in a hopeless or angry stance in life. Recognizing devaluing attitudes is the first step; deciding individually what to do about them is a second step.

Chris is a white woman at the beginning of the process of developing an identity as a lesbian. She presents a familiar picture of some women who come out as lesbians in their 40s to 50s who have previously stayed away from intimate contact with others. She has a complex pattern composed of a self-identity that is isolated and independent, a recently emerging need to be deeply connected with others, and an awareness that such connection is going to be as a lesbian. When she thinks of lesbians, she has in mind a combination of stereotypes she sees as negative, including butch, ghetto mentality and high visibility (politically active). She internally experiences this shift in identity as mandating her to leave behind her identity as a teacher, a lover of good food and classical jazz, and her heterosexual friends. She is needing to absorb an individual identity as someone who is both independent and connected and to integrate that fuller vision of herself with her identity as a member of the group, lesbians. Through her therapy, she is able to talk about her stereotypes and begin to look beyond them for real people. She started first with reading, particularly anthologies written about lesbians which gave her some insight into differences. She then attended a coming-out workshop for lesbians new to the process. But a major shift occurred when she attended a party with other lesbians and experienced first-hand the ways they were "just people," like her in many ways and different from each other and any of the stereotypes she had.

INTEGRATION OF POSITIVE DOMINANT GROUP IDENTITY WITH INDIVIDUAL IDENTITY

Members of dominant groups do frequently identify with particular groups in society, but they do not usually identify with the groups through which they are dominant. For example, in this country, when asked to identify by race/culture, white people usually identify the European culture from which they descend. What they do not usually do is identify as white no matter how long their families have been in the United States. Psychologically, this may be a two-fold process. People do try to group themselves based on what they see that makes them different from the people around them. To most people, the concept of group means a sub-group of the majority—something small enough to embrace. Secondly, those of us who are members of dominant groups live and breathe that as the norm. We don't even think to pull it to the foreground as relevant; our white skin, our heterosexuality, our physical ability are so much like the air we breathe that we don't consciously see them (Helms, 1990; Kivel, 1996; Tatum, 1993).

The times when dominant characteristics are clear ways of defining oneself, they are most often used consciously to reinforce the dominance. White supremist groups certainly see themselves as white and use that to fight physically and psychologically to stay dominant. Heterosexuality has been in the social and political arena lately and is used to deliberately and actively punish/devalue homosexuals. Some men in describing their view of a good way to be male, still define it, in part, as being superior to female, rather than finding a new definition not built on devaluing women (Hagan, 1992).

There are personal and societal ramifications of continuing to render invisible one's dominant status. A critical consequence is confounding the particular with the universal. In other words, if people don't see themselves as white, for example, and therefore do not clearly understand how being white has affected their beliefs, attitudes, values, and behaviors, they are at risk for generalizing their personal experiences to all others and assuming it is a universal one. White feminists have experienced this generalization around gender. White males have been the norm and universal standard against which all others have been judged. This rendered white female experience invisible, not studied, not used as a basis for developing good psychological theory, for example, until the last twenty-five years. The privilege and power over others that comes with dominance ranges from not having to attend to being male or white, for example, to projecting your life attitudes onto all other people, to actively building a life around the dominance of others. In this country, being white, male, heterosexual, able-bodied, and middle-class are dominant positions with the power to presume their way of being is best and consequently to render being people of color, female, homosexual, disabled, and working class or poor invisible (Adelman & Enguidanos, 1994; Comas-Diaz & Greene, 1994; Hill & Rothblum, 1996).

To develop a positive, contextual identity that includes various dominant group identities necessitates that an individual claim her/his dominant status, recognize it as particularistic, and develop a dominant identity that is built on valuing individuals in non-dominant status. Some racial identity theorists have described the development of a positive white racial identity that is not built upon the devaluing of people of color (Helms, 1992). In *A Race Is a Nice Thing to Have,* a book she wrote for white people, Helms (1992) captures the essence of this in her title. According to Helms, a process of developing a positive white identity involves understanding racism, choosing to confront it, and developing an identity built on seeing color in people (including white) and choosing diversity in one's life. Neither process would allow for settling for guilt or withdrawal, saying "this is just the way I am." A parallel process has been identified by others (Garcia, 1995; Hagan, 1992) and can be adapted for social class, physical ability or any other grouping in which the dominant position is defined, in part, by devaluing of the minority position.

Integrating a positive dominant group identity into a sense of self provides for a solid awareness of one's own context. The lack of such grounding takes an individual out of context and thereby, automatically, places too much emphasis on either an individual identity (I am smart) or on a particular group identity (women) and doesn't balance those with other identities (white).

Liz and Mary, as white heterosexual women with friends who are lesbian, both expressed some envy of lesbians who have a group to belong to that seemed to provide a built-in base for the development of friendships and broader networks. Liz has been very involved for decades in a wide range of political activities including Black civil rights work and support for lesbians and gay men. She talks about how hard it is for her to experience a sense of community with other white, heterosexual women and men since she sees herself as markedly different from most of them. Mary eventually came out as a lesbian and believes she has found not only a partner and friends, but a sense of community, a home. Both of these women have experienced the isolation of being without group identities which they value. They were/are thrown back on only their personal connections with other individuals and not a sense of a broader something to which they belong.

Sam is a 75-year-old retired professor who is married for the third time, this time to a woman who is very sensitive to the privileges attached to being male. Sam has decried male authority for a long time, sees himself as a peacemaker, and has traditionally feminine aspects to his personality. At the same time, he does move through the world as a white male, sometimes oblivious to his own behavior. His way of handling this in the past was to try to deny his maleness, to almost refuse to identify with it, wanting to identify with women instead. In this case, Sam's seeing himself as different from others in the group "male" and like some in the group "female" has been very emotionally problematic for him. He still struggles with who he is as an individual and who he is as a man.

INTEGRATION OF DIFFERING GROUP IDENTITIES

Sophie is a 30-year-old doctor who has strong cultural identities sometimes at conflict with her individual identity. She was raised in a Jewish family with cultural and religious traditions with which she very much identifies. She has incorporated her Jewish identity into her adult life in ways congruent with her lesbian identity, which is also very strong. She now lives several states away from her family of origin and has spent much of her 20s learning about how she personally feels and thinks, what she wants to do as work, and what part of her past she wants to bring into the present and what she doesn't. Most of the time, she moves with ease among her various worlds and has done a wonderful job of integrating them.

At times, though, she experiences conflict between identities. For example, her family of origin has strong expectations of Sophie as a Jewish daughter. These role behaviors are important not only to her parents and extended family, but to Sophie as well. She likes being the good daughter in those particular terms. However, at times, those expectations are in strong conflict with her individual needs, particularly when she is overworked or wanting to stay at home and celebrate holidays. This is not just a conflict between her parents' desires and her own, nor is it a conflict between how she thinks she should be and how she is. It is clearly a conflict between two different ways of defining herself. She is a Jewish daughter and she is an individual with individual needs. Another form of conflict arises for her between the two group identities of Jewish and lesbian. Sometimes, those identities work well together, but trouble emerges for her when, for example, members of her extended family do not accept her lesbian partner at family occasions. She is pushed to choose between what she sees as valuing her life as a lesbian and valuing her life as a caring adult, contributing to family celebrations.

Claire is a 60-year-old Catholic nun who has lived all her adult life within a religious community. She has worked in a variety of settings with a wide range of responsibilities all within the aspirations and structure of her religious order. She still holds deeply to the goals and ideals of her community, but has within herself begun to realize that the hierarchal structure has severe limitations and negative consequences for her personally. She has found it helpful to sort through her conflict by understanding that the core problem for her personally is not simply the structure of the organization, but rather the internal push and pull about how she views herself if she doesn't accept the structure. She has tried on many occasions to alter the structure somewhat and will continue to do so. However, at present, she has to find a way to have her identity as a nun and her identity as a feminist with her own ideas of how to be of service to others.

Nancy had been politically active as a lesbian-feminist during the 70s and early 80s. She saw herself as part of a larger lesbian cultural and political community that was very important to her. In the mid-80s, she felt that the purpose had gone out of her political action. She withdrew from many cultural events and directly stated that she no longer knew where she belonged. She experienced an extreme sense of loss and isolation with the dissolution of the sense of purpose she shared with many others. She has never replaced that sense of belonging with anything else. A few years ago, Nancy was diagnosed with multiple sclerosis. Her physical health was a series of exacerbations and remissions which left her unable to count on her physical ability at any given point in time. In spite of being a health care worker herself, a participant in various support groups across the years, and a believer in group identity, Nancy had a very difficult time coming to see herself as an individual with MS and furthermore, as some-one with a physical disability. When she could begin to accept herself as disabled, she began to attend support groups and to make personal connec-tions through those networks, decreasing her isolation. She talked about the difficulties within herself as ones of identity—who is she and where does she belong?

COMMUNICATION BETWEEN PEOPLE WITH DIFFERENT GROUP IDENTITIES

Learning how to communicate across various group identities is a criti-cal aspect of relating, particularly when communicating between dominant and minority positions. Maria Lugones (1990), in her article "Playfulness, 'world'-travelling, and loving perception" provides an excellent frame for understanding how to do this. A "world" in her sense can be extrapolated to mean group identity. Based on her ideas, travelling, with care, would be cultivated as a positive way to be. People in minority positions usually live in both dominant and minority worlds and therefore know the language, customs and norms of both groups. People in dominant positions in soci-ety do not have to travel. White people can stay within the white world, for example, feeling at ease there, and never have to venture into the worlds of

Blacks, Mexicans, or Chinese people in the United States. Positive portrayals of minority worlds are not fully visible on television or in the paper. So many novels are written from a white perspective that one can choose never to read about people of color. White people can go to meetings on end without having to be the only white person in the room. This means, in order to understand truly the worlds of minorities, we have to make the effort to become "biculturally competent" (Garcia, 1995).

Judy came from a childhood filled with chaos resulting from alcoholism, violent behavior, and mental illness of family members, erratic and unexplained absences of siblings as they were sent to Boys Town or juvenile detention facilities, and lack of economic and social resources to help with some of the problems. Her coping style was to be quiet, trying to scan and fix everyone to minimize the chaos. She, herself, had not had problems with alcohol or drugs, though she had been in relationships where she had been emotionally and verbally abused. She was ashamed of her childhood life and found it hard to talk to me about it. She accurately saw me as someone with a background different from hers. As we talked about the differences between us, she was able to see her history as a "world" she could let me into, one that I was willing and able to travel to with care. During therapy, she developed a new relationship with a woman. As she told bits and pieces of her history to her new partner, her partner became scared that the chaos Judy talked about would erupt in their relationship. Talking about her background as a culture of chaos and violence compounded by poverty helped Judy and her partner both see that though this was the "world" Judy came from, it was not synonomous with the individual personhood of Judy. They both could begin to separate out the individual identity of Judy and the group identity of Judy. Her new partner could also see the importance of talking about her own background as particular to herself and others raised like her, and not a universal standard against which all other families were compared. Talking about the differences also helped Judy see that claiming her background, rather than rejecting it out of shame, did not mean she was trapped in it. It was a world in which she had lived, and still travelled at times when she visited with various family members. She was also contructing a different world for herself in the present.

Judy learned to integrate a group identity into her relationship. Other couples can get stuck on understanding the group identity and need to move to a more individual identity to connect with each other. Sarah and Diane are a lesbian couple who have been partners for several years. They are very different on many dimensions including degree of outness about their lesbianism, introversion and extraversion, and valuing of emotionality. These differences are imbued with cultural ones as well. Sarah was born and raised in Peru, had been married and has three children. Her siblings, aunts and uncles, children and grandchildren live nearby and she has accepted the mantle of family matriarch, consistent with her standing in her family. Diane was raised in white, Southern United States Baptist culture valuing emotional and financial independence and self-sufficiency. Both understand clearly the cultural differences between them and how, in their particular cases, that affects them personally. The cultural differences are striking and respected by both Sarah and Diane, yet they frequently feel at a loss on how to bridge them. In therapy, they have had to shift from the discussion of culture onto what is, for them, a harder arena of individual feelings, needs and desires. For example, they need to focus on feeling abandoned or lacking power. When they can do this, they usually find the way to move forward.

Heterosexual couples can illustrate a familiar pattern of using group status as both an excuse and a weapon. Leigh and Jack illustrate both sides of this. Leigh says Jack is too limited in his emotional range, unable to communicate with her the way she wants—he is such a classic man. Jack's comparable statement is that Leigh is far too emotional, swings from one extreme to another, and gets too lost in her navel-gazing. He sees her as a typical woman in these ways. Both statements are name-calling, condescending of the other person, and a sure way to either stop the conversation or escalate a circular fight. Both Leigh and Jack also use their group identity as male or female as an excuse for their own behavior. Jack says "I am a man and that way (talking about emotions) is not natural for me." Leigh says "I have no interest in superficial ways of interacting; I am only interested in more intimate connections." Both use their cultural (male and female) upbringing as a way to say "This is how I am and I cannot change." Shifting out of these positions of being stuck within a particular group identity has necessitated getting back to individual identity. As they talk about what they are thinking and how they are feeling, they open to the connection possible between them in a way that acknowledges their differences. They will always have their gender differences but, by filtering these through their unique selves, they are able to find an intimate way to cross the gap.

INTO THE ARENA OF SOCIAL CHANGE:
BEYOND IDENTITY POLITICS

The social milieu, including patterns of power based on dominant and minority positions, affects and creates some of our individual psychological patterns, a fact that feminist therapists and others have been discussing for a long time. In part, that milieu of the United States reinforces limited identity development. In dialogues, in the media, in personal, professional and social settings, people frequently put forth only one form of identity. We argue with each other over whether or not we are more alike or different as people, whether we should be responded to as individuals or as members of a group, and how our personal patterns are or are not representative of a particular group pattern. We use those views to justify patterns of domination or to explain how we think those patterns can be changed. These discussions take place in a cultural context that values independence and individualism, dualistic thinking and a power-over mentality. This atmosphere leads toward either/or thinking, an over-reliance on individual effort and abusive power arrangements.

Given this social context, people may choose one primary way to understand themselves. When people choose individuality as the main way to define themselves, they lose grounding and embeddedness and see themselves as far too important. They are at risk for personalizing everything, good and bad, that happens. Especially when a person in the dominant position in society emphasizes individuality, she/he believes she/he arrived there by virtue of his/her particular efforts and believes others should be able to do the same, even when oppression and prejudice exist. In a minority position in society, someone who focuses on individuality is also at risk for personalizing the world. A societal problem, e.g., homophobia, which is a reaction to a group of people, can be absorbed as a personal problem, even if the recipient understands it is the others who are homophobic.

When an individual absorbs a group identity as the primary way of seeing oneself, she/he gives up a sense of uniqueness, a sense of self that sees oneself as different from others of that cultural group. At the same time, a totally group-defined individual loses the clear, full understanding of how others not of the group are very much like her/him.

Psychology has a responsibility to help create a different social milieu. Just as the social context creates individual psychological patterns for people, so the individual psychological patterns can create the social milieu. As therapists, we can contribute to a change in social context through a conscious attending to the frame we choose for personal identity. The therapy relationship itself becomes a model of relating through our varied contexts (Brown, 1994). In addition, the effects of a shift in thinking about identity can begin to spill over into the lives of ourselves and our clients beyond the therapy room.

In the video, *Both of My Moms' Names Are Judy,* children ages 7-12 talk about their experiences in school with regard to having lesbian and gay parents. The children are very articulate about the minority group with which they identify and about the homophobic school system and how that can make life difficult for them. They understand that the problems are group based, though they affect them individually. Two of the older students initiate talking to various classes about the behavior of the students and how it is hurtful to them. The students they talk with change and the school setting is therefore somewhat better. Though the video is designed as a teaching tool for educators and not as an example of psychological processes, it illustrates the impact on the next generation of a new consciousness and the ability to shift between individual and group identities.

A psychological shift into an understanding of identity as contextual and multileveled can be brought into the social change arena as well. Instead of holding discussions from an either/or position and arguing about whether it is more important to be seen as an individual or a member of a group, the focus can be shifted to both/and. For example, Kim attended an open meeting to discuss racism in the lesbian and gay community. The room was filled with people with African, Central and South American, Asian and European ancestry. Some speakers from racial minorities spoke about the importance of group identity while others said they were just individuals. White speakers usually spoke about the importance of being seen and seeing others as individuals. Kim, wanting the discussion to be inclusive of both positions, asked that speakers begin their statements with the phrase "As a white (or Asian or Hispanic, etc.) lesbian or gay man, I think . . . " Since this was a discussion about race, this phrase helped each speaker particularize, rather than generalize their own position, while still emphasizing the individuality of what was being said.

CONCLUSION

As feminist therapists, part of our responsibility is to contribute to changing the social environment which is partially responsible for creating the limited psychological patterns of ourselves and our clients. One way to do this is to be conscious of the theoretical beliefs we hold and to continuously choose understandings that work toward full integration of people. The Western theoretical concept of identity has had a hole in it regarding full integration of group identity into the understanding of an individual. As we continue to use a more complex understanding of identity in our work with individuals, those individuals will carry that fuller construct into their roles as parents, partners, teachers and social change agents.

REFERENCES

Adleman, J. & Enguidanos, G. (Eds.). (1994). *Racism in the lives of women.* New York: The Harrington Park Press.

Barrett, S. (1990). Paths toward diversity: An intrapsychic perspective. In Brown, L. & Root, M. (Eds.). *Diversity and complexity in feminist therapy.* Binghamton, NY: The Harrington Park Press.

Brown, L. (1994). *Subversive dialogues: Theory in feminist therapy.* New York: Harper Collins.

Comas-Diaz & Greene, B. (Eds.). (1994). *Women of color: Integrating ethnic and gender identities in psychotherapy.* New York: The Guilford Press.

Garcia, M. (1995, November). *Bicultural competence.* Presentation at Advanced Feminist Therapy Institute. Albuquerque, NM.

Hagan, K.L. (Ed.). (1992). *Women respond to the men's movement.* San Francisco, CA: Pandora.

Helms, J.E. (1992). *A Race is a nice thing to have.* Topeka, KS: Content Communications.

Helms, J.E. (Ed.). (1990). *Black and White racial identity: Theory, research and practice.* Westport, CT: Greenwood Press.

Hill, M. & Rothblum, E. (1996). Classism and feminist therapy: Counting costs. *Women & Therapy, 18,* 3/4.

Kivel, P. (1996). *Uprooting racism: How White people can work for racial justice.* Philadelphia, PA: New Society Publishers.

Lesbian and Gay Parents Coalition International. (1994). *Both of my moms' names are Judy.* (Available from Gay and Lesbian Parents Coalition International, 4938 Hampden Lane, #336, Bethesda, MD 20184).

Lugones, M. (1990). Playfulness, "world"-travelling, and loving perception. In Anzaldua, G. (Ed.). *Making face, making soul* (pp. 390-402). San Francisco, CA: Aunt Lute Books.

Tatum, B. (1987). *Assimilation blues: Black families in a White community.* Westport, CT: Greenwood Press.

Tatum, B. (1993). *Racial identity development and relational theory: The case of black women in white communities.* Wellesley, MA: The Stone Center Work in Progress Series. (Serial No. 63).

Japanese Feminist Counseling as a Political Act

Masami Matsuyuki

SUMMARY. This article presents a brief review showing that feminist therapy has been a political act in North America historically, theoretically, and practically. Within this framework, the author gives the history and the cultural context of Japanese feminist counseling in relation to Eastern thought and to women's liberation movements with a focus on three key concepts, "independence," "dependence," and "maternity." She provides information about the Japanese Association of Feminist Counseling Practices and Studies as a political turning point for Japanese feminist counselors. Their definitions and implementations of an essential feminist belief that "the personal is political" are examined and then are illustrated through consciousness-raising groups, networking, attempts at influencing public policy, and challenges to professionalism. *[Article copies available for a fee from The Haworth Document Delivery Service: 1-800-342-9678. E-mail address: getinfo@haworth.com]*

Masami Matsuyuki, BA, is a Japanese graduate student in Women's Studies at Mankato State University with a research emphasis on feminist counseling.

The author wants to acknowledge the support for this article by Japanese feminist counselors and members of the Japanese Association of Feminist Counseling Practices and Studies.

Address correspondence to: Masami Matsuyuki at 33-16 Tsunoekita-machi, Takatsuki-shi, Osaka 569, Japan.

[Haworth co-indexing entry note]: "Japanese Feminist Counseling as a Political Act." Matsuyuki, Masami. Co-published simultaneously in *Women & Therapy* (The Haworth Press, Inc.) Vol. 21, No. 2, 1998, pp. 65-77; and: *Feminist Therapy as a Political Act* (ed: Marcia Hill) The Haworth Press, Inc., 1998, pp. 65-77; and: *Feminist Therapy as a Political Act* (ed: Marcia Hill) The Harrington Park Press, an imprint of The Haworth Press, Inc., 1998, pp. 65-77. Single or multiple copies of this article are available for a fee from The Haworth Document Delivery Service [1-800-342-9678, 9:00 a.m. - 5:00 p.m. (EST). E-mail address: getinfo@haworth.com].

© 1998 by The Haworth Press, Inc. All rights reserved.

WOMEN'S LIBERATION MOVEMENTS
AND FEMINIST THERAPY IN NORTH AMERICA

Feminist therapy has been a political act: Feminist therapists proclaim that women are not sick, but society is. In North America, feminist therapy has a historical, theoretical, and practical base for this position.

The literature (Enns, 1993; Sturdivant, 1980) suggests that feminist counseling/therapy had two major historical backgrounds. One source was the rise of humanistic psychology and radical psychiatry and therapy which supported feminist critiques of the androcentric, in other words, the women-as-deficiency model of psychology (e.g., Miller, 1976; Weisstein, 1971), of psychiatry (e.g., Chesler, 1972; Wyckoff, 1977), and of psychoanalysis (e.g., Chodorow, 1978; Millet, 1969). The pervasion of sexist bias among mental health professionals was confirmed (Broverman, Broverman, Clarkson, Rosenkrantz, & Vogel, 1970); and feminist therapists eventually indicated that even humanistic therapies which put the focus on individual growth in the existing society were not satisfactorily effective for women (Greenspan, 1983). The other and more direct source was the second-wave women's liberation movement itself. Specifically, the term "feminine mystique" (Friedan, 1963) drew publicity to the distress of women living in a sexist society. Then, the impact of consciousness-raising groups on women led to the development of feminist agencies, including feminist therapy collectives.

The basics of feminist therapy theories redefined the concepts of "therapy," "power," and "politics." Therapy was understood as a healing and consciousness-raising process toward action (Mander & Rush, 1973), and the principles (sharing and change-orientation), processes (sociopolitical analysis of women's experiences and resocialization), and goals (sisterhood and social change) of consciousness-raising groups were analyzed (Brodsky, 1977; Kirsh, 1974; Kravetz, 1980) and were integrated into therapy. Differences in power were described as "power over" and "power within" (Smith & Douglas, 1990). Women's awareness of "power within" themselves was expressed as "empowerment" which affirmed individuals to be strong, whole, and active (Mander, 1977) so that they could "define/change the world" (Burstow, 1992, p. 2). In connections with women, empowerment is mutual, developing understanding and empathy among them that bridge their individual experiences toward action (Siegel, 1990; Surrey, 1991). Politics was redefined by feminists as "one's relationship to power" (Mander & Rush, 1973, p. 51). The politics in feminist therapy meant "making connections between the inside world and the outside world" (p. 18), in other words, the integration of personal and political dynamics which coexist in women's lives (Gilbert & Rossman, 1993).

Feminist therapists perceived social changes as occuring in two interdependent dimensions. As individual women change their consciousness and live "in a way that is already changed" (Hill, 1990, p. 64), they are changing society (Mander, 1977; Greenspan, 1983; Worell & Remer, 1992). At the same time, feminist therapists and clients take actions outside of therapy in various ways in their alliance with women's liberation movements. Social changes are necessary in order to accomplish radical changes in women's lives (Espin, 1993; Rosewater, 1984; Sturdivant, 1980). Actually, women's involvement with activism can be therapeutic in terms of recognizing their skills and abilities and finding alternative options through the examples of other women's lives; also, feminist therapists who take risks and leadership in political actions are role models for women (Gluckstern, 1977).

Many feminist therapists have taken political actions, such as conducting feminist action research, providing public services and education which embody feminist philosophy, coordinating support groups within community, influencing public policy, advocating women as expert witnesses, and working with grass-roots organizations (Enns, 1993). Feminist therapists are envisioned as midwife or teacher rather than surgeon or scientist (Chesler, 1989). With making more effort toward theorizing the experiences of women who come from different life backgrounds and encounter multiple oppressions (Brown & Root, 1990; Comas-Diaz & Green, 1994; Kanuha, 1990), feminist therapy will expand still more its potential for being a political act. Feminist therapists can be political activists who act on their feminist beliefs and values for the healing, empowerment, and sisterhood of women.

WOMEN'S LIBERATION MOVEMENTS AND FEMINIST COUNSELING IN JAPAN

In contrast to feminist therapy in North America, Japanese feminist counseling was formed separately from women's liberation movements in Japan, at first (Japanese Association of Feminist Counseling Practices and Studies, 1994a). Kawano Kiyomi, who had been a clinical social worker in Japan, worked and studied in the United States from the late 1960s through the 1970s. When she returned to Japan, she introduced feminist therapy to her colleagues and opened *Feminist Therapy "Nakama"* [Companions] in Tokyo in 1980 (Kawano, 1986).

In the late 1970s, the outcomes of women's liberation movements in

Japan were surfacing in society, having been accelerated by the announcement of the Japanese government's domestic action plans formulated for
the United Nations Women's Decade. The media incited confusion among
Japanese women facing a reconsideration of traditional feminine roles and
the potential for more choices; they sent double messages to women that
"women's independence [an expected characteristic of women with ca-
reers] is in," and "old maids [how women with worthwhile careers sup-
posedly end up] will not have a happy life after all." Both full-time
housewives who believed in traditional feminine roles of being wife and/
or mother and single women who had no adequate alternative role models
in their lives fell into identity crises (Japanese Association of Feminist
Counseling Practices and Studies, 1993; Matsubara, 1988).

This phenomenon had a commonality with the issues identified in *The
Feminine Mystique* (Friedan, 1963) and in *The Cinderella Complex*
(Dawling, 1981) in the United States. White middle-class American
women as portrayed in those books and Japanese women who had been
influenced by feminism were similar in terms of their social status due to
their class and ethnic privilege. However, the concepts of "independence," "dependence," and "maternity," all of which are interrelated
with "femininity," and the context of Japanese women's conflicts concerning those concepts are different from, and more complicated than
those for White American women.

The concept of "dependence" for the Japanese is deeply embedded in
Eastern thought and is a key to understanding the Japanese sense of self
(Rosenberger, 1992). The teachings of Buddhism and Zen regarding "no-
self" (Suler, 1993) and the unity of all living and material objects (Kondo,
1988) enhanced a Japanese culture that valued harmony, "maternity," and
"dependence." Those aspects of the culture penetrated Japanese psycho-
analytic theories, such as the *Ajase* complex (Kosawa, 1933, cited in
Okonogi, 1971) and *amae* theory (Doi, 1971). They were developed based
on two male psychoanalysts' understanding of relationships between a
mother and a child and the significance of *amae*, which more recently
refers to the multifaceted and interactional dependence for human development in the Japanese context (Taketomo, 1986). *Amae* creates attach-
ment and connections to others but often does so along with a sense of
obligation to others. "Independence" in a Western sense is considered
"selfish," that is, as attempting to be free from any sense of obligation. A
form of "independence" accepted in the process of human development in
Japan is called *jiritsu*, "socially sensitive independence" (Kamitani,
1993). Generally, more men than women are encouraged to attain it.

The issues concerning "independence" and "maternity"/"motherhood" in relation to "femininity"/"womanhood" have been constantly addressed in women's liberation movements in Japan (Fujimura-Fanselow & Kameda, 1995). A profound conflict for Japanese feminists has been how to challenge traditional feminine roles that are restrictive for women without losing the support of family/community ties, which offer both social stability in life and a kind of "sisterhood" existing due to a strict gender segregation. "Maternal" values have been often co-opted by the patriarchal/androcentric base of Japanese culture, such as the *tenno* [Japanese emperor] system and the *ie* system [Japanese patriarchy derived from Confucian feudalism], and they have been exploited to uphold the systems of oppression, putting women in no-win situations. Therefore, Japanese feminists have consciously emphasized the importance of women's "independence."

Thirteen years after the emergence of feminist counseling in Japan, the Japanese Feminist Counseling National Conference was held in Osaka in 1993. Then, the Japanese Association of Feminist Counseling Practices and Studies was organized. (This is the only feminist association for counselors and their allies in Japan, but it does not represent all Japanese feminist counselors.) Japanese feminist counselors began networking, theorizing their experiences, and reflecting on their relationships to women's liberation movements and their implementation of a belief that "the personal is political." Japanese feminist counselors have attempted to incorporate this essential feminist belief into their counseling practices. I distributed a questionnaire from December of 1996 to February of 1997 and conducted an interview in February of 1997 to gather information about feminist counseling in Japan, and one feminist counselor responded, "if a counselor thinks that it is impossible [to act on the belief], she is not practicing feminist counseling."

Japanese feminist counselors' definitions regarding the belief that "the personal is political" in their responses to the questionnaire, to the interview, and in the literature (Human League, 1995) can be summarized: many women's problems are caused by oppressive social systems; it is important to accept women's distress that is rooted in social injustice and to tell women that this is not their fault; it is empowering to realize that an individual woman's problem is shared by many women; and personal change ultimately makes social change. Many Japanese feminist counselors share the viewpoint that feminist counseling should aim at both personal and social changes (Inoue, 1993).

The responses of Japanese feminist counselors to the questionnaire and the interview indicate that they have implemented their belief that "the personal is political" in the following ways: practicing counseling based on feminist values such as empathy toward and affirmation of women, reconsideration of gender roles, and mutual empowerment for social change; working toward changing oppressive social systems by supporting women's groups outside of counseling; and serving as role models, living as change agents.

The membership of the Japanese Association of Feminist Counseling Practices and Studies (1994b) exhibits the enthusiasm of feminist counselors and their allies for supporting women in social change. They state that:

1. The Japanese Association of Feminist Counseling Practices and Studies is a group of people who hope that women can enjoy living who they are as individual human beings, who consider the conditions of women's psychological problems and their social backgrounds, and who support women to solve problems and/or to recover from them.

2. The members of this association understand the mistakes and defects in conventional counselings in terms of their practices and their "professionalism." In order to establish feminist counseling by women for women, they intend to share ideas that can be effective, to create theories, to reflect on practices, and to take actions. Also, they are willing to communicate and cooperate with one another regardless of their affiliation with any existing schools of psychology or their status as professional or amateur.

3. The members of this association attempt to be free from hierarchical and authoritative structures that exist in current society. Therefore, they do not have a representative or a "head." Administration is maintained by diverse and equally concerned individuals' commitment and their mutual consent. By discussing, reflecting on, and acting on their thoughts with one another, the members aim at enhancing themselves and bringing about social change.

The participants in the Japanese Feminist Counseling National Conference are counselors/therapists from different training backgrounds: grass-roots feminist activists, doctors and medical staff, public servants, social workers, students, and teachers. In order to make the best use of the diversity of people who are interested in this association, the administration committee of 1996 proposed a variety of networks for support and action, including a geographic regional network, a network based on interests, a network based on workplaces, a network of non-practitioners, a counseling-referral network, a grass-roots women's network, and a daily support network (Japanese Association of Feminist Counseling Practices and Studies, 1996b).

The contents of conferences described in their reports reflect the members' interests and the participants' concerns for Japanese feminist counseling, including theorizing Japanese feminist counseling, clarifying differences in the conditions and problems of feminist counseling in public and private practices, raising people's awareness of the pervasion of sexual violence against women and children, and learning group approaches and techniques. They also encourage exploring prominent counseling issues for women in Japan, such as eating disorders, alcohol dependency, mother-daughter and father-daughter relationships, concepts of independence and dependence, climacteric and ageism for women, women's bodies, sexuality/eroticism, and lesbianism.

Japanese women's conflicts are often expressed more inwardly and somatically according to a set of behaviors considered to be socially appropriate for women (Japanese Association of Feminist Counseling Practices and Studies, 1994a). Some feminist counselors interviewed point out that Japanese women who seek counseling are generally lacking a sense of self and self-esteem and express high levels of stress because they cannot "depend" on anyone. While *amae* is regarded as a more feminine and/or childlike characteristic, traditional feminine roles as caretaker oblige them to fulfill others' emotional needs first, leaving their own needs for last.

Feminist counselors who support women's "independence" are viewed as "political" in Japan. Conventional therapeutic communities once criticized feminist therapists whom they believed "commercialize" and "minimize" psychotherapy by appealing to women's independence, search for identity, and assertiveness, taking advantage of a social trend in the 1980s. What this criticism implies is that encouraging and "spreading an illusion" of women's independence is dangerous to society (Hirakawa, 1992, p. 31). Yet, with knowing women's "independence" as a key for the wellness of Japanese women and social change, Japanese feminist counselors remain committed to promoting consciousness-raising groups, self-assertion training, and self-esteem enhancement training for sharing knowledge and skills and helping women to learn to take leadership and to form their own groups.

In the process of theorizing Japanese women's experiences in consciousness-raising groups (Japanese Association of Feminist Counseling Practices and Studies, 1995a), some Japanese feminist counselors found that a pattern in those groups was a weak sense of self in a Western sense and continued reliance on "dependence" and "sisterhood" in a Japanese sense, that is, a form of "we are all the same and together." In contrast to feminist therapists' reconsideration of independence toward interdependence in the West (e.g., Bradshaw, 1990; Eichenbaum & Orbach, 1983;

Jordan, Kaplan, Miller, Stiver, & Surrey, 1991), this is the reason that Japanese feminist counselors put more emphasis on "independence" for Japanese women and on a need for the transformation of Japanese "sister-hood."

Japanese feminist counselors have started to work more closely with women consultants in public facilities, the staff in public women's centers, and grass-roots feminist groups. Such networking is vital for the empow-erment of women in Japan because they can share the merits and greatly compensate for the demerits of each workplace with one another. Women consultants in public facilities have worked with a large number of women, not only Japanese but also Koreans and Asian migrants in Japan who are typically economically more oppressed and consequently have had little access to private counseling services. Women consultants also have more advantage than most feminist counselors in their connections to various public facilities; however, they have to cope with institutions without a sense of "human rights" for women (Japanese Association of Feminist Counseling Practices and Studies, 1995a). For example, a woman consultant revealed that there must have been a pile of records in public facilities regarding sexual violence, forced prostitution, hardship of Asian migrant women, abortion by teenage girls, and women's poverty (Japanese Association of Feminist Counseling Practices and Studies, 1995a), which had not been openly discussed in public before feminists pointed out those issues.

Public women's centers usually can afford a wider range of services than grass-roots groups and private practitioners, and above all, most of their services are free. One prefectural women's center offers services including: a library on women's issues; conference rooms available for groups concerning women's issues; cultural, educational, and skill-build-ing programs; and counseling programs. Their counseling programs con-tain not only individual counseling but also legal and health consultations, feminist counseling courses, self-assertion training, and support groups in Japanese, Korean, Chinese, and English. However, many public women's centers have ended up ignoring the priority of women's needs in each community. For example, some feminist groups claim that the establish-ment of shelters and crisis centers is more urgent than educational pro-grams in women's centers because the number of public and private shel-ters in Japan is extremely limited (Uno, 1997).

The staff in one private shelter states that their small shelter has always been busy responding to the referrals from public facilities with little financial backup from the government. One of their concerns is that home-less women who need intensive mental health care are often transferred from one public facility to another and in the end return to their shelter. Such women are severely economically oppressed and neither recognize their ill condition nor a need for counseling because of their immediate survival needs (Japanese Association of Feminist Counseling Practices and Studies, 1995a). Grass-roots groups which were developed as women's health centers and rape crisis centers have financial problems as well, and they experience limitations of activities. Lesbian and bisexual feminist groups confront additional difficulty in attempting to organize because of heterosexism in Japanese society.

Japanese feminist counselors are becoming active in influencing public policy. For example, they held a workshop at the non-governmental organization forum of the International Women's Conference in Beijing (Japanese Association of Feminist Counseling Practices and Studies, 1996a); organized a mental health care team in Takarazuka after a devastating earthquake in the Hanshin area of Japan in 1995 in order to respond to the survivors' needs (Japanese Association of Feminist Counseling Practices and Studies, 1995c); sent a request to the Japanese government to establish a law to inhibit violence against women by the year 2000 (Japanese Association of Feminist Counseling Practices and Studies, 1995a); and supported a women's group dealing with a sexual harassment case (Japanese Association of Feminist Counseling Practices and Studies, 1995b). Their attempts at legal advocacy have just begun and have not been successful because Japanese feminist counselors are not regarded as "professional" (Japanese Association of Feminist Counseling Practices and Studies, 1996c).

Japanese feminist counselors challenge "professionalism" and licensure. The Ministry of Health and Welfare is planning to establish a national licensing system for counselors. This would exclude many Japanese feminist counselors with comparatively fewer academic credentials from being considered as "professional." They are also limited by the lack of Japanese feminist counseling literature and the uncritical use of Western concepts in Japanese therapeutic communities in general. Establishing systematic training programs based on Japanese women's experiences will be one of the many important issues in Japanese feminist counseling.

REFERENCES

Bradshaw, Carla K. (1990). A Japanese view of dependency: What can amae psychology contribute to feminist theory and therapy? In Laura S. Brown & Maria P. P. Root (Eds.), *Diversity and complexity in feminist therapy* (pp. 67-86). New York: The Harrington Park Press.

Brodsky, Annette M. (1977). Therapeutic aspects of consciousness-raising groups. In Edna I. Rawlings & Dianne K. Carter (Eds.), *Psychotherapy for women: Treatment toward equality* (pp. 300-309). Springfield, IL: Charles C Thomas Publisher.

Broverman, Inge K., Donald M. Broverman, Frank E. Clarkson, Paul S. Rosenkrantz, & Susan R. Vogel. (1970). Sex-role stereotypes and clinical judgments of mental health. *Journal of Consulting and Clinical Psychology, 34*(1), 1-7.

Brown, Laura S. & Maria P. P. Root (Eds.). (1990). *Diversity and complexity in feminist therapy*. New York: The Harrington Park Press.

Burstow, Bonnie. (1992). *Radical feminist therapy: Working in the context of violence*. Newbury Park, CA: Sage Publications.

Chesler, Phyllis. (1972). *Women and madness*. New York: Doubleday.

Chesler, Phyllis. (1989). *Women and madness*. San Diego: A Harvest/HBJ Book.

Chodorow, Nancy. (1978). *The reproduction of mothering: Psychoanalysis and the sociology of gender*. Berkeley: University of California Press.

Comas-Diaz, Lillian & Beverly Greene (Eds.). (1994). *Women of color: Integrating ethnic and gender identities*. New York: The Guilford Press.

Dawling, Colette. (1981). *The Cinderella complex: Women's hidden fear of independence*. New York: Summit Books.

Doi, Takeo. (1971). *"Amae" no kozo* [Anatomy of "dependence"]. Tokyo: Kobundo.

Eichenbaum, Luise & Susie Orbach. (1983). *What do women want: Exploding the myth of dependency*. New York: Coward-McCann.

Enns, Carolyn Zerbe. (1993). Twenty years of feminist counseling and therapy: From naming biases to implementing multifaceted practice. *The Counseling Psychologist, 21*(1), 3-87.

Espin, Oliva M. (1993). Feminist therapy: Not for or by white women only. *The Counseling Psychologist, 21*(1), 103-108.

Friedan, Betty. (1963). *The feminine mystique*. New York: A Laurel Book.

Fujimura-Fanselow, Kumiko & Kameda Atsuko (Eds.). (1995). *Japanese women: New feminist perspectives on the past, present, and future*. New York: The Feminist Press.

Gilbert, Lucia Albino & Karen M. Rossman. (1993). The third decade of feminist therapy and the personal is still political. *The Counseling Psychologist, 21*(1), 97-102.

Gluckstern, Norma B. (1977). Beyond therapy: Personal and institutional change. In Edna I. Rawlings & Dianne K. Carter (Eds.), *Psychotherapy for women: Treatment toward equality* (pp. 429-444). Springfield, IL: Charles C Thomas Publisher.

Greenspan, Miriam. (1983). *A new approach to women & therapy*. Blue Ridge Summit, PA: TAB Books.

Hill, Marcia. (1990). On creating a theory of feminist therapy. In Laura S. Brown & Maria P. P. Root (Eds.), *Diversity and complexity in feminist therapy* (pp. 53-66). New York: The Harrington Park Press.

Hirakawa, Kazuko. (1992). Feminist therapy: Arinomamano jibun wo koteisuru-koto no konnanna jidai ni mukete [For the age of difficulties in affirming themselves]. In Hamamatsu Josei no tame no Counseling Room (Ed.), *Josei no shakaika sodachiai o mezashite: Grow up movement . . . hand in hand* (pp. 31-35). Hamamatsu.

Human League (Ed.). (1995). *Josei no tame no counseling joho '96-'97* [Information about counseling for women]. Tokyo: Chihaya Shobo.

Inoue, Mayako. (1993). Feminist counseling: Dentoteki counseling to kotonaru shiten towa? [What are viewpoints that are different from those of traditional counseling?]. *Rinshoshinrigaku Kenkyu* [Studies of Clinical Psychology], *31*(2), 35-41.

Japanese Association of Feminist Counseling Practices and Studies. (1993). *Feminist counseling national conference report*. Osaka.

Japanese Association of Feminist Counseling Practices and Studies. (1994a). *Feminist counseling national conference report*. Osaka.

Japanese Association of Feminist Counseling Practices and Studies. (1994b). *Membership for Japanese Association of Feminist Counseling Practices and Studies.* [Leaflet]. Osaka.

Japanese Association of Feminist Counseling Practices and Studies. (1995a). *Feminist counseling national conference report*. Osaka.

Japanese Association of Feminist Counseling Practices and Studies. (1995b). *Feminist counseling news*, *2*(5). Osaka.

Japanese Association of Feminist Counseling Practices and Studies. (1995c). *Feminist counseling news*, *2*(6). Osaka.

Japanese Association of Feminist Counseling Practices and Studies. (1996a). *Feminist counseling news*, *2*(8). Osaka.

Japanese Association of Feminist Counseling Practices and Studies. (1996b). *Feminist counseling news*, *2*(9). Osaka.

Japanese Association of Feminist Counseling Practices and Studies. (1996c). *Feminist counseling news*, *2*(10). Osaka.

Jordan, Judith V., Alexandra G. Kaplan, Jean Baker Miller, Irene P. Stiver, & Janet L. Surrey. (1991). *Women's growth in connection: Writing from the Stone Center.* New York: The Guilford Press.

Kamitani, Yukari. (1993). *The structure of jiritsu* [socially sensitive independence] in young Japanese women. In *Psychological Reports*, 72, 855-866.

Kanuha, Valli. (1990). The need for an integrated analysis of oppression in feminist therapy ethics. In Hannah Lerman & Natalie Porter (Eds.), *Feminist ethics in psychotherapy* (pp. 24-36). New York: Springer Publishing Company.

Kawano, Kiyomi. (1986). Feminist Therapy "Nakama" no kaisetsu [Opening Feminist Therapy "Companions"]. In Kiyomi Kawano, Kazuko Hirakawa, Shigeko Koyanagi, & Reiko Yamazaki, *Feminist therapy* (pp. 39-56). Tokyo: Kakiuchi Shuppan.

Kirsh, Barbara. (1974). Consciousness-raising groups as therapy for women. In Violet Franks & Vasanti Butle (Eds.), *Women in therapy: New psychotherapies for a changing society* (pp. 326-354). New York: Brunner/Mazel Publishers.

Kondo, Akihisa. (1988). *Bunka to seishinryoho/Nihonjin to shizen* [Culture and psychotherapy/Japanese and nature]. Tokyo: Sanno Shuppan.

Kravetz, Diane. (1980). Consciousness-raising and self help. In Annette M. Brodsky & Rachel T. Hare-Mustin (Eds.), *Women and psychotherapy: An assessment of research and practice* (pp. 267-281). New York: The Guilford Press.

Mander, Anica Vesel. (1977). Feminism as therapy. In Edna I. Rawlings & Dianne K. Carter (Eds.), *Psychotherapy for women: Treatment toward equality* (pp. 285-299). Springfield, IL: Charles C Thomas Publisher.

Mander, Anica Vesel & Anne Kent Rush. (1973). *Feminism as therapy*. New York: Random House.

Matsubara, Junko. (1988). *Croissant shokogun* [The Croissant syndrome]. Tokyo: Bungeishunju.

Miller, Jean Baker. (1976). *Toward a new psychology of women*. Boston: Beacon Press.

Millet, Kate. (1969). *Sexual politics*. New York: Avon Books.

Okonogi, Keigo. (1971). Nipponteki seishinbunseki no kaitakusha Kosawa Heisaku [The founder of Japanese psychoanalysis Kosawa Heisaku]: Ajase complex. In Takeo Doi & Keigo Okonogi (Eds.), *Gendai no espuri: Seishinbunseki* [Contemporary espirit: Psychoanalysis] (pp. 227-232). Tokyo: Shibundo.

Rosenberger, Nancy R. (Ed.). (1992). *Japanese sense of self*. Cambridge: Cambridge University Press.

Rosewater, Lynne Bravo. (1984). Feminist therapy: Implications for practitioners. In Lenore E. A. Walker (Ed.), *Women and mental health policy* (pp. 267-279). Beverly Hills: Sage Publications.

Siegel, Rachel Josefowitz. (1990). Turning the things that divide us into strengths that unite us. In Laura S. Brown & Maria P. P. Root (Eds.), *Diversity and complexity in feminist therapy* (pp. 327-336). New York: The Harrington Park Press.

Smith, Adrienne J. & Mary Ann Douglas. (1990). Empowerment as an ethical imperative. In Hannah Lerman & Natalie Porter (Eds.), *Feminist ethics in psychotherapy* (pp. 43-50). New York: Springer Publishing Company.

Sturdivant, Susan. (1980). *Therapy with women: A feminist philosophy of treatment*. New York: Springer Publishing Company.

Suler, John R. (1993). *Contemporary psychoanalysis and eastern thought*. New York: State University of New York Press.

Surrey, Janet L. (1991). Relationship and empowerment. In Judith V. Jordan, Alexandra G. Kaplan, Jean Baker Miller, Irene P. Stiver, & Janet L. Surrey (Eds.), *Women's growth in connection* (pp. 162-180). New York: The Guilford Press.

Taketomo, Yoshihiko. (1986). Amae as metalanguage: A critique of Doi's theory of amae. *Journal of the American Academy of Psychoanalysis, 14*(4), 12-17.

Uno, Sumie. (1997). What are women's centers in Japan? In Dawn Center (Ed.), *Dawn: Newsletter of the Dawn Center* (Osaka prefectual women's center). Osaka.

Weisstein, Naomi. (1971). Psychology constructs the female, or the fantasy life of the male psychologist. In Michele Hoffnung Garskof (Ed.), *Roles women play: Readings toward women's liberation* (pp. 62-83). Belmont, CA: Brooks/Cole Publishing Company.

Worell, Judith & Pam Remer. (1992). *Feminist perspectives in therapy: An empowerment model for women.* Chichester, England: John Wiley & Sons.

Wyckoff, Hogie. (1977). *Solving women's problems: Through awareness, action & contact.* New York: Grove Press.

Politicizing Survivors of Incest and Sexual Abuse: Another Facet of Healing

Jo Oppenheimer

SUMMARY. As both a feminist therapist and a survivor of incest, moving myself beyond therapeutic issues into an area of public education has been crucial to my own healing process. Receiving positive responses to my workshops and discussion groups, it became apparent that using a similar approach with clients who were survivors might be beneficial to their healing. As a member of The Counseling Center for Women, a feminist therapy collective in Israel, I suggested we sponsor a public exhibition and a series of programs of the topic of incest and abuse. The Municipality of Tel Aviv was approached to be its governmental sponsor. Entitled "Silent No More," the program moved therapists and clients from working in the privacy of therapy to a public forum. What began as an uncomplicated educational program became an emotional process and a politicizing of individuals to help others as well as themselves. Moving from a feeling of shame to a sense of empowerment, the exhibition gave us a new sense of self-esteem and strength in our own abilities and our recovery process. *[Article copies available for a fee from The Haworth Document Delivery Service: 1-800-342-9678. E-mail address: getinfo@haworth.com]*

Jo Oppenheimer, MA, is a clinical psychologist in Israel where she was one of the Founders of The Counseling Center for Women, a feminist therapy collective. She specializes in working with survivors of sexual abuse and incest. She is presently in the United States attending the Women's Therapy Centre Institute in New York City while maintaining a private practice.

Address correspondence to: Jo Oppenheimer, 298 Mulberry Street, Apartment 5L, New York, NY 10012. Electronic mail may be sent to (Listen3rd@aol.com).

[Haworth co-indexing entry note]: "Politicizing Survivors of Incest and Sexual Abuse: Another Facet of Healing." Oppenheimer, Jo. Co-published simultaneously in *Women & Therapy* (The Haworth Press, Inc.) Vol. 21, No. 2, 1998, pp. 79-87; and: *Feminist Therapy as a Political Act* (ed: Marcia Hill) The Haworth Press, Inc., 1998, pp. 79-87; and: *Feminist Therapy as a Political Act* (ed: Marcia Hill) The Harrington Park Press, an imprint of The Haworth Press, Inc., 1998, pp. 79-87. Single or multiple copies of this article are available for a fee from The Haworth Document Delivery Service [1-800-342-9678, 9:00 a.m. - 5:00 p.m. (EST). E-mail address: getinfo@haworth.com].

© 1998 by The Haworth Press, Inc. All rights reserved.

79

This article addresses my own experiences as I moved from confronting my issues as an incest survivor with a feminist therapist to incorporating feminist therapy principles as I worked with other women survivors of incest and sexual abuse. My becoming a political activist on behalf of survivors of incest and sexual abuse stemmed from my rage at having been victimized for years, not only by my abuser, but by the society in which I had grown. "Only pain, anger and distress make us politically active" (Sender, 1992, p. 256).

In this article I will present a specific illustration that gave my clients, myself, as well as others, the opportunity to speak out about incest and sexual abuse in a public forum, thereby empowering ourselves and furthering our healing process. To understand how this action came about, we must briefly examine feminist therapy itself.

Feminist therapy is a multifaceted approach to the therapeutic process. Its core, however, incorporates a philosophy that therapy explores individual issues within a "broader social framework" (Brown, 1992, p. 243). The goal of feminist therapy is to create change through empowerment. For women, often disenfranchised by the society in which they live, empowerment includes promoting social change through political action (Brown, 1992). Our first responsibility is to allow clients "to speak, in their own voices, naming their own experience[s] and realities" (Brown, 1996, p. 12). The client is the expert. An interactive approach, an important facet of feminist therapy, allows our values to be stated and modeled. As Patricia Spencer Faunce (1985) states: "Women's experiences are shared by every woman and are therefore political. What was thought to be a personal problem has a social cause and . . . a political solution" (p. 313). These experiences are grounded in a patriarchal society in which women, and children, are treated as chattel. A woman's "distress while unique within her experience . . . " results from "coping with a dominant culture which wishes to render women invisible. . . . " (Brown, 1992, p. 245).

Healing from the individual abuse and acknowledging the wider scope "of oppression, disempowerment, and violation that an adult survivor may have experienced" (Brown, 1996, p. 12), feminist therapy with survivors of incest and sexual abuse adds a further dimension to the therapeutic process. Incest is the ultimate violation of the child's trust and love. It takes advantage of the child's naturally powerless position to destroy her sense of self. Defenses such as dissociation and denial, originally adapted to protect the core self, become maladaptive and problematic in adulthood. Healing incorporates not only struggling with individual issues but also "the struggle to change the conditions that caused or contributed to . . . victimization" (Russell, 1995, p. 432). However, it must be recognized that not every client wants or needs to be a political activist. Moving from the safety of a two-person therapy to the wider scope of a public forum may not be a possibility. Although I believe it adds an important component and creates another facet in the progression of healing, I must also be willing to let my clients define their own healing process.

The Counseling Center for Women (TCCW), a feminist therapy collective, was formed in Israel in 1986. For one year we familiarized one another with our theoretical and therapeutic ideology. In 1987, we opened two Centers–first in Tel Aviv and the second in Jerusalem–offering feminist therapy to women, their significant others and their families. We continued to meet weekly as our in-house training gave us the opportunity to explore topics reflecting our personal expertise.

TCCW was the only organization in Israel to specialize in feminist therapy for adult survivors and to recognize that "[t]he crucial element of incest and sexual abuse is not what occurred but its impact on the individual" (Gil, 1983, p. 19). Although many of our clients had been in therapy before coming to TCCW, few of their previous therapists had experience with this population. Either their issues had not been addressed or they were recognized but their importance was disavowed.

Until TCCW began to collect statistics for our total number of adult survivors in therapy, little hard data on this population existed in Israel. For the years between 1991-1993, 50% of all our clients were survivors. In 1997, the incidence continues at 48%.

Our work with survivors, combined with our in-house workshops, led members of the collective to increased knowledge and greater expertise. We soon realized that we had important information to share outside of the collective with other mental health professionals. We expanded our in-house workshops to include other therapists and we presented lectures at: the Bar-Ilan School of Social Work where a special course for social workers working for Israeli municipalities was offered; for Masters students attending the Wertzweiller School of Social Work; for women connected to the Women's International Zionist Organizations (WIZO) in Jerusalem; and, for volunteers at the Feminist Centers in both Tel Aviv and Haifa. This was the beginning of the collective's political activism in a society whose religious and philosophical tenets reflected the patriarchy. Incest was a forbidden topic.

My political activism began approximately two years after acknowledging my own personal history of incest in therapy. My therapist encouraged me to employ my knowledge as both client and therapist to educate others publicly. The process began gradually. I presented workshops within the collective. Surrounded by friends, I was able to articulate issues about incest and sexual abuse within a supportive milieu from both a personal and professional perspective.

While my own recovery continued to take place, a change in the public sector was also occurring. In 1988, Israeli television aired the American film "Something About Amelia." It was the first time television presented the issue of incest publicly. Because the showing of the movie resulted in a flurry of phone calls to rape crisis centers and child abuse centers throughout Israel, the media focused their attention on the topic for a brief period. All forms of childhood abuse were beginning to be recognized as a growing problem. Governmental and private programs expanded to provide better care for children who suffered abuse but adults, who endured abuse as children, were largely ignored.

By 1992, the collective recognized it was time to bring the topic of adult survivors and its ramifications to the attention of the general public. As a survivor, I understood that an important component of my healing process had been to address the issues publicly. I envisioned a multi-media exhibition that would include both professionals and clients and began the process to make it a reality.

Israeli therapists, with whom we had previously networked, were contacted. They and their clients were invited to participate. The therapists were requested to join us as panel participants, sharing their therapeutic expertise. Unfortunately, the response was less than overwhelming. Perhaps they felt uncomfortable with airing the topic or with being political or with speaking about it with their clients. Though a few therapists outside of TCCW did volunteer to participate, the majority of the therapists and survivors who took part in the exhibition were from the TCCW Centers and the Rape Crisis Center of Tel Aviv.

We contacted the municipality of Tel Aviv to enlist local governmental support of the project. After prolonged negotiations, two sites were offered: the main floor of City Hall for an art exhibition, and the Cinematheque, a theatre owned by the city, where a variety of programs addressing abuse would take place on two consecutive evenings.

In January 1993, the work of fourteen artists opened at City Hall and the Cinematheque. The title "Silent No More" expressed the political nature of the exhibition. Each artist wrote a short explanation of her work, elaborating on the individual pieces as works of art as well as part of her healing process. Both exhibition sites featured black poster-board covered with articles from the Israeli Hebrew and English newspapers on the subject of incest, sexual abuse and rape. Our purpose was to show how prevalent abuse was in our society.

At the Cinematheque several organizations that worked with similar populations established information booths and distributed literature on services they provided. TCCW therapists and counselors from the Tel Aviv Rape Crisis Center were available to answer questions and provide crisis intervention at both sites.

The first evening at the Cinematheque, several videos of interviews with incest survivors were shown. An art therapist, who specialized in working with survivors of incest and sexual abuse, showed slides of her clients' work, discussing both their meanings and their healing properties. The evening concluded with a panel of therapists from throughout Israel discussing issues previously raised.

Survivors and a few volunteers were involved in all stages of the planning and production of the live performances that took place the second evening. A play written specifically for the exhibition was performed by the playwright and other survivors. The play was followed by live readings of poetry by seven survivors. For several of the performers, reading their own work proved too difficult. The women solved their dilemma by exchanging their work with other performers, thereby participating but not reading their own emotionally charged work. As the initiator of the exhibition, observing them problem-solve and protect themselves confirmed the experiential growth and healing for individual survivors. The performances were followed by a panel of TCCW therapists, specializing in incest and sexual abuse. Various issues, including the importance of the entire program, were discussed, thus ending the second evening.

Over 100 people attended each night, a considerable number for Israel. The impact on those in the audience became apparent when, at the end of both evenings, a number of women came forward to talk with TCCW members, the performers and with me. Many were identifying themselves as survivors for the first time publicly. They were grateful that these issues were finding a public platform.

The overall publicity before and after the program was extensive. The media–television, radio, newspapers and magazines–discussed the issues of incest and sexual abuse, interviewing members of TCCW and the Tel Aviv Rape Crisis Center. Speaking as both a therapist and a survivor, I was interviewed for a television news program and a woman's magazine. In addition, I exhibited photographs and art work produced as a component of my therapy. Obviously, it was *my* healing time, too.

The programs and the accompanying publicity resulted in women reaching out to TCCW and to Rape Crisis centers in Israel. Eleven calls were received by TCCW within a week following the conclusion on the exhibit. My willingness to speak publicly as a survivor of incest brought about nine phone calls from men and women who never had revealed their abuse before speaking with me.

Immediately after the completion of the exhibition and programs, the Haifa Rape Crisis Center expressed an interest in having a similar exhibition there. TCCW, Jerusalem, began to plan their own exhibition. Women from the incest survivor's support group at the Tel Aviv Rape Crisis Center began brainstorming about possible outreach to the public, as both individuals and a group. The Rape Crisis Center began an Organization for Survivors and a Friday morning open group to which anyone could come. Together, the Rape Crisis Center and TCCW, Tel Aviv, planned to initiate additional programs that would meet client needs. TCCW offered more workshops for professionals and continued its outreach at the university level.

It was, however, the impact on the individuals who participated throughout the programs that was the most profound. The following are quotes taken from a series of telephone interviews conducted in 1997. I chose two of my own ex-clients with whom I have maintained contact and who continued to be politically active. The third woman, Tamar (all names have been changed), was a colleague's ex-client who was politically active before and after the exhibition.

> The positive was that I was included in a group process which left me being not so alone; not so secretive. There was something very healing about the process.

> It reinforced that I was not alone. We've hidden all our lives; been ashamed all our lives. It gave incredible reinforcement as to what we all had to deal with. How brave we are in dealing with it.

> The need to tell the world that these things really happen appeared to me to take priority.

Tamar was one of the few participants who had spoken publicly before the exhibition. She shared with me why she had appeared on television without a disguise.

> I decided that if I am going on in a disguise, I'm sending out a message: "Hey, girl, you've got to hide." I didn't want survivors seen as a strange race; as someone who had something wrong with them. We are a part of society.

Participating in the exhibit was another vital component to her sense of self, to her healing process.

It was almost as though I had this disease that nobody could know about. We've hidden all our lives; kept it hidden all our lives; been ashamed of it all our lives. It has to be known that it happens, happens often and to a lot of people. It's not only up to us to take care of it. Society has to take care of it. It's a public menace. It's no less a crime than murder. It murders our soul and our very being.

Naomi was the only participant who was abused by her mother. Angered by the fact that abuse by women was never dealt with by the media, she nonetheless felt empowered through her participation. That she was able to connect to other survivors was critical.

I was able to meet other women, other survivors. The Rape Crisis Center formed an Organization of Survivors and had open Friday morning meetings that I attended for a while. That felt really good.

Ofra not only exhibited her paintings but, for the first time, she proudly signed them.

I had to stand behind what I wanted to exhibit. The way for me to do it was to avoid my past actions and sign the paintings. I knew I was exposing myself but it felt important to do this.

In addition, Ofra wrote the play that depicted her experience of abuse.

My openly participating was a way to tell my personal story. But it was not just my story. I wanted to show the public what happens to young girls and boys. I wanted to reach the professionals in whose hands are the tools to identify these girls and boys.

Only Tamar referred directly to the political nature of her participation,

I gave lectures on incest and incest survival. Each time at least three women came forward to tell me about themselves. It was confirmation for the need; that it has to come out of the closet in which "These things don't happen in Israel." That's political.

Clearly, all the participants were being political, their participation signifying their need to change society. It was apparent to the women that the exhibition was part of their healing process. "Becoming an activist can be therapeutic in a very different way . . . as well as contributing to the social healing" (Russell, 1995, p. 433).

The exhibition took over eight months of planning, from its conception to its completion. It brought together women's organizations from all over Israel who contributed time and money. Mental health professionals were provided with information on professional and personal levels. The life-long effects of incest and childhood sexual abuse were dramatically communicated. The public became aware of the devastation of abuse. Most of all, it empowered survivors who worked directly on the project, providing us with a public voice as well as offering another facet of healing.

Political action is often only associated with elections and other governmental actions. There are, however, other forms of action, more personal, that are political in nature and whose purpose is to effect direct social change. As early feminists declared: "The personal is political." When we begin to heal and speak out, in a society that denies the existence of incest and the damage it causes, "[w]e reach back to those who are still trapped in . . . continued abuse" (Ellison, 1997, p. 13).

Through our participation and exposure, we discovered, as Tamar stated, "How brave we are in dealing with incest publicly." We were neither "the only one" nor powerless. We had created a political forum by which we confronted the ignorance and secrecy that existed in our society. "Political movements consist of people in agreement that something needs to be changed. People then take action to create that change" (Ellison, 1997, p. 13).

Through political action, we freed ourselves, discovering strength and pride. We empowered ourselves to move on in new directions.

In conclusion, creating the exhibition presented me with a unique opportunity. As a political activist, I was able to involve the city of Tel Aviv to publicly support the exhibition. In addition, women's organizations were brought together, contributing to a sense of camaraderie as we worked toward a common goal. As a therapist, I was able to encourage clients in a political action that furthered their healing. As a client, I was also able to "reach back" and help myself and others to come forward and be silent no more.

REFERENCES

Brown, L. S. (1992). While waiting for the revolution: The case for a lesbian feminist psychotherapy. *Feminism & Psychology, 2*(2), pp. 239-253.

Brown, L. S. (1996). Politics of memory, politics of incest: Doing therapy and politics that really matter. *Women & Therapy, 19*(1), pp. 5-18.

Ellison, K. L. (1997, January-February). Coming into consciousness as a movement. *The Healing Woman, 5*(9), pp. 13-14.

Faunce, P. S. (1985). Teaching feminist therapies: Integrating feminist therapy, pedagogy & scholarship. In L. B. Rosewater & L. E. A. Walker (Eds.), *Handbook of feminist therapy: Women's issues in psychotherapy.* New York: Springer Publishing Company.

Gil, E. (1983). *Outgrowing the pain.* New York: Dell Publishers.

Russell, D. E. H. (1995). Politicizing sexual violence: A voice in the wilderness. *Women & Therapy, 17*(3/4), pp. 425-434.

Sender, K. (1992). Lesbian therapy and politics: Inclusion and diversity in observations and commentaries. *Feminism & Psychology, 2*(2), pp. 255-257.

Border Crossing
and Living Our Contradictions:
Letters Between Two Feminist Therapists
About Doing Therapy with Men

Nayyar S. Javed
Nikki Gerrard

SUMMARY. Diversity has become a buzzword in the public discourse on today's world. In this article we talk about diversity within men's sense of self, and the repression of their sense of self by the imposition of a socially constructed "masculinity."

Men who come for therapy in our clinic are often marginalized because they have trouble in assimilating to the cultural norms of patriarchy. Our ongoing discussions about the pains of men who resist a seductive social representation has helped us to identify our own dilemmas.

Our feminist perspectives, in terms of social, political, and economic analyses, led to a new paradigm in which to view our male clients. While we acknowledge a vast diversity in how men deal with

Nayyar S. Javed, MEd, is a social activist and a feminist therapist in Saskatoon Adult Community Mental Health Services. Dr. Nikki Gerrard, PhD, is a community psychologist and social activist as well as Head Psychologist at Saskatoon Adult Community Mental Health Services.

Address correspondence to: Nayyar S. Javed and Nikki Gerrard at Saskatoon District Health, 4th Floor, Birks Building, 165-3rd Avenue South, Saskatoon, Saskatchewan, Canada, S7K 1L8.

[Haworth co-indexing entry note]: "Border Crossing and Living Our Contradictions: Letters Between Two Feminist Therapists About Doing Therapy with Men." Javed, Nayyar S., and Nikki Gerrard. Co-published simultaneously in *Women & Therapy* (The Haworth Press, Inc.) Vol. 21, No. 2, 1998, pp. 89-100; and: *Feminist Therapy as a Political Act* (ed: Marcia Hill) The Haworth Press, Inc., 1998, pp. 89-100; and: *Feminist Therapy as a Political Act* (ed: Marcia Hill) The Harrington Park Press, an imprint of The Haworth Press, Inc., 1998, pp. 89-100. Single or multiple copies of this article are available for a fee from The Haworth Document Delivery Service [1-800-342-9678, 9:00 a.m. - 5:00 p.m. (EST). E-mail address: getinfo@haworth.com].

© 1998 by The Haworth Press, Inc. All rights reserved.

89

self's diversity, we have chosen to talk about two specific ways many of our male clients contain it. In this article, we track these issues and this journey toward a new paradigm based on feminist analyses, our politics and our separate social locations in society as a racialized woman (NJ) and as a white woman (NG). Our personal struggles of raising our sons and our professional work with male clients is described in order to shed light on "border crossing and living our contradictions." *[Article copies available for a fee from The Haworth Document Delivery Service: 1-800-342-9678. E-mail address: getinfo@haworth.com]*

Dear Nikki,

As a racialized woman and often doing therapy with white men, I have to make myself step out of the bounds of the two socially constructed identities that simultaneously intersect with each other and generate intersubjectivity both in me and my clients, that arises out of the colonial images of the racialized women and images of women created by patriarchy for supporting itself.

My work with male clients is a continuous struggle of what bell hooks (1994) conceptualizes as "border-crossing." The border which I must cross has been erected by colonialism and patriarchy to confine racialized women by constructing "femininity" and "people of colour" as the "other" of the real people. This portrayal of "other" as an aberration of humanity has an enormous salience in my work as a therapist. Similarly, identifying the presence of my "otherness" in my relationship with my male clients and challenging it with utmost subtlety and caution so that I don't damage the relationship with them is political work. It often takes its toll but sometimes there are rare rewards that I find in the sparse compliments I receive from my male clients.

Another facet of my political work is helping them also to engage themselves in resisting the seductions of "masculinity" and freeing themselves of the shame they experience as a consequence of seeing themselves as lacking the ideals of masculinity. So my work constitutes border crossing at many levels. I do it by resisting gendered and racialized identity. Similarly my clients also move out of their male identity by embracing their "otherness" as something to celebrate, because being the "other" of socially constructed masculinity frees them to recognize their inner diversity–the various parts of self that constitute the totality of an individual.

Many of my male clients are experiencing otherness partly because they do not have jobs or have low-paying jobs. They are economically disadvantaged and are made to feel responsible for it because they are seen as lacking what it takes to be real men. I find a feminist critique of patriarchy and capitalism an extremely useful tool in reframing the problem. But I often go beyond reframing in search of uncovering those parts of the self that are gendered by patriarchy and devalued by patriarchy and capitalism. The devaluation of those parts of self forces men to live a life in self-alienation. While many men who succeed in fitting the ideals of masculinity go on living in this state without much anxiety, the men who do not see themselves as successful in this regard are the ones who have trouble, though at the unconscious level.

Nikki, I find myself border crossing in proposing this theory. I am neither a theoretician nor am I a scholar, so this theory has plenty of ground for lacking plausibility, and therefore, its rejection. However, I am not giving up because of the fear of its rejection because fortunately, I know men, through literature in Sufism (the mystic tradition of Islam), who have dared to not only acknowledge but also nurture their inner-diversity. These men have lived their lives by engaging in an ongoing project of "Knud Agahi" or the search for finding, acknowledging and nurturing the self's diversity. Crossing the border, i.e., the bounds of gender-based definitions of self, is a major part of their work (Shafi, 1985).

Their female counterparts such as Ribbia of Busraa, a renowned Sufi woman, join in this endeavour (Nurbacksh, 1983). They have gone beyond the restrictiveness of "femininity" and have been encouraged by their male co-workers. Gendering self and humanity has been something they have resisted in the search of communion with the "Creator," who is also freed from gender categories in the Sufi discourse. The distinction between the representations of "Him" or "Her" are often very tenuous in the Sufi discourse.

Many Sufi scholars like Rumi the Persian (Arastch, 1965) have developed quite comprehensive theories of self and have seldom devalued those parts of self that are attributed to femininity. In fact, the parts of self that patriarchy values in men are the ones Sufis try to subdue by seeking communion with the "One" who is "Creativity, Love and Rahmat (or eternal blessings)."

Carl Jung (1968) seems to have reached a similar state of mind in his conceptualization of human psyche as a constellation of archetypes. Thus he has acknowledged self's diversity and also validates "the feminine" as an integral part of psyche's structure. But in depicting the feminine, Jung has often turned to the mythical images of women that represent women as vicious seductresses. Moreover, Jung's portrayal of the feminine is deeply embedded in the oppositional thinking perpetuated by patriarchy to deval-ue women (Romaniello, 1992).

Jung's thoughts have evolved in a cultural context that rewards men for self's alienation from "the feminine." Jung deserves some credit for being able to capture a glimpse of the feminine within his own psyche but did not dare to nurture it. He resorted to betrayal, thus abandoning the task of the self's discovery at a full scale. I turned to Jung with hopes but did not find what I was looking for.

So, I turned to some of my male clients who have helped me in recog-nizing self's diversity by opening up their inner world to me and leading me to see the glimpses of what Sufis have revealed in their work on understanding self. My clients' angst of self-alienation and shame for failing to achieve masculinity has reinforced my belief in and commitment to doing the political work of border crossing both at personal and societal levels. I find that the struggle of individuals border crossing within them-selves requires immense energy, energy that exists within human beings but is invested in repressing those parts of self that are gendered for men and women. Alienation from those parts is abundantly rewarded in men by patriarchy and capitalism. Despite the seduction of these rewards, some men are not willing to live a life of self-alienation and make a conscious decision to resist the pressures of conforming. The signs of their resistance to this seduction may be present at a very early age. My own son surprised me at age 14 by resisting a role model whom I thought would help him succeed in life.

I took my young son to a distant city to meet a cousin of mine who is a very eminent and successful scientist. I have admired this man for many years and looked up to him as a mentor. I was eager for my son to meet him, hoping that some of this man's brilliance would turn a light on in my son's life and that the two of them would connect. After my son spent some time with my cousin, I later asked him what he thought of this man. "His face was crooked, Mom," was all that he had to say about my cousin, much to my shock, disappointment, and despair.

Only later did I realize that I wanted my son to see this man through *my* eyes, which is not only an impossibility but not particularly healthy either. I also realized that my eyes looked through a lens that was formed by religion, patriarchy and capitalism. My cousin, despite his support of feminism, and the recognition of self's diversity, epitomizes the patriar-chal image of a man whose creativity is invested in serving patriarchy, capitalism, and religion.

My son continued his struggles to keep consciously getting attached to those parts of self that removed him from stepping into the bounds of an identity that forces self-alienation. His struggles were not painless, either for him or his father and myself. We had difficulties in allowing him to cross the borders that restrict men within the confines of the socially constructed masculinity. But the process of finally letting go of our own hang-ups strengthened my realization of the existence of self's diversity and the pressures on men to give it up. It also made me realize the embeddedness of my thoughts in patriarchy and the work I have to do to transcend those oppressive gender categories that define humans. The realization that I was manipulating my son to follow a "successful male role model" has been a positive outcome of the pain I experienced because of my son's resistance to what I was coercing him to do.

My observations of how men deal with self's diversity have clearly pointed out variations in the knowledge of its presence and handling the emotional consequence of its containment. The psychological work invested in containing it goes on at various levels of awareness. I have seen clients who are quite aware of this diversity but have internalized its devaluation by society. They are conflicted and experience tension because of the social oppression that does not allow the expression of diversity and imposes "otherness" on its consequences. The desire to give up self's diversity clashes with an equally important pull for keeping all parts of self alive. For these men, making the changes needed to fit the norms of masculinity is an arduous task and is often thwarted.

Then there are men who have adopted a course of development that has forced them to repress their diversity. They have little awareness of its existence and invest an incredible degree of psychological energy in proving themselves to be "men." The fear of not fitting the ideals of masculinity and the seduction of the rewards for uncritically embracing it force them to develop an elaborate system of defensive mechanisms. They think nothing of committing violence against women and often come for therapy either for stress-related health problems or more recently for perpetrating violence.

I will share a case history with you to illustrate the type of men who are aware of the diversity of self and have trouble in repressing its existence. For the purpose of confidentiality, I will call him Mr. K and make some minor changes in his biographical information.

Mr. K grew up in a small town. His mother left his father when Mr. K was six years old. He moved away with her. His relationship with his step-father was quite turbulent but there was no physical abuse.

Mr. K was a laid-back child. He did not have many friends and was quite isolated and withdrawn. But he was quite bright and as the years went on, he became very good at expressing his creativity through writing.

He was not interested in the activities most boys pursue as a way of learning the ropes necessary for masculinity.

He was absorbed in his own world and kept writing. He attempted suicide at age twenty-one and since then has been seeing a psychologist and psychiatrist for "obsessive compulsive disorder" for a number of years.

He came to see me at age thirty-five and I have been seeing him for a few years. I often feel extremely impressed by his brilliant insight and its reflection in his writing. But the conflict between the desire to keep alive all parts of his self, and the seduction of giving up those parts of self that defy the ideal of masculinity, consumes all of his energy and he continues to experience depression. His depression seems to arise out of the internalized devaluation of his self's diversity. There are times when he comes very close to embracing it and finally makes a statement to validate its presence. But he lives in a world that reinforces his shame for not fitting male norms. The containment of diversity during those moments becomes awfully burdensome.

His painful struggle to accept himself and to take the lid off the containment of his diversity has engendered a deep sense of powerlessness. The need to transform those social structures that have necessitated this struggle becomes apparent. I realize that no amount of "reframing" is going to help him in accepting his diversity. He is paying a huge emotional cost along with material disadvantages.

This realization often creates those moments of self-doubt I experience in doing therapy in the systems that are so deeply entrenched in patriarchy. This realization, however, is necessary for doing the political work feminists of the world talked about when we met in Beijing for the Fourth International Women's Forum in 1995. We challenged patriarchy and its institutions by articulating the need for a paradigm shift in managing our lives, society and the globe. We demanded "looking at the world through women's eyes" because it is necessary for achieving peace, equality and development.

I believe "looking at the world through women's eyes" will require intense work at the individual level. Men and women have to work together for the transformation of the world and both men and women need to acknowledge, value and develop those parts of self that constitute "women's eye." Sufis have conceptualized those parts as love, creativity and Rhmat (a constellation of attributes required for kindness. I can find no word in English which can capture its meanings). In simple terms, it means empathy, connectedness and capacity to give. Unfortunately, in the Eurocentric models of psychology, giving is not valued. Similarly, empathy and connectedness can be hurtful to capitalism and its agenda of globalization. For the world trade order, one loses in a big way by adhering to these attributes. Nevertheless, the need for empathy and connectedness for achieving peace and stopping violence against our planet is simply too intense to be ignored. Similarly, the need to recognize self's diversity and its capacity for empathy is equally important for the achievement of inner peace and for stopping violence against the gendered parts of self in developing paradigms of masculinity.

Feminist therapy is an important part of consciousness raising about the dangers of monolithic self. Monolithic self is an empty shell that expresses its inner turmoil through obsessive-compulsive feelings, thoughts and behaviour. At the social level, individuals in the position of power deal with their anxiety by filling the emptiness with alcohol, greed and violence. Patriarchy and capitalism create this emptiness because they work to subjugate women, the colonized and poor. The result is the collective amnesia that Saul (1995) describes as manifested in "the creation of a civilization that scorns knowledge of itself" (p. 3). Resistance to the emptiness of self is a political task we, as feminist therapists, must pursue with our male clients.

As feminist therapists, we have been engaged in working with women's loss of their self's diversity but, somehow, we have left men out. I hypothesize that we, as feminist therapists, exercise a gender difference in dealing with the sense of emptiness that is caused by repressing the inner diversity. Power differences play a role here: many men express this emptiness by turning to violence–psychological, sexual and economic. We need to draw men into our struggle for shifting paradigms of relationship with self, others and the world or we will not go very far. When self's emptiness is experienced by a man, in a position of power, its expression changes–it erupts in violence.

I have hope that some day Mr. K will succeed in looking at himself "through women's eyes" and allow himself to develop his diversity. But I am not sure about the men who have no desire to look at those parts of the self that frighten them.

What do you think about all this, Nikki?

Your friend,

Nayyar

* * *

Dear Nayyar,

I live my contradictions. I have just read your letter and it has evoked contradictory thoughts in me and I want to run them by you and see what comes of it, as we so often do with each other.

One of my reactions when I read your letter was, "Oh no, not again! Not women twisting themselves into pretzels in order to take care of men!" Yes, I agree that there are many men who do not ascribe to the values of patriarchy, who have "feminine" characteristics, who have been ostracized and labelled and punished because of it. Some of these men end up at the clinic where we work. They are troubled and defeated and often depressed. They feel worthless and helpless. They often are resigned to living in poverty and social isolation. When you and I talk about these men, we feel for them, we struggle with where to go with them on their journey of seeking a happier place. That is the one side of my experience with these men.

On the other side is my knowledge about patriarchy, about women as socially constructed to have enormously less power than men in the Big Three arenas: social, political and economic. I know about women's socially assigned roles of World Nurturer, Caregiver, Mother, Mom, Ma to earth, country, community, family, children. I know the price women pay for these roles: those losses of power in the Big Three plus the emotional costs: depression, anxiety, mania, panic, phobias, other mental illness labels. I know the labels that women get: enmeshed, controlling, schizophrenogenic, masochistic and so on. And these are the nicer labels. I know all these things. You know all these things. This is basic Feminism 101 stuff.

And this knowledge comes to visit me when I read in your letter about "crossing borders"; what happens to us when we work with men. When this knowledge visits me I want to scream "So What? Who's job is it to save men from themselves?" Let these men suffer in their own juice of patriarchy. When they hurt badly enough, perhaps they will do something about it. The operative word here is "they." Not us.

On the other hand (yes, now we have 3 hands) there are our sons. We began to cross the border the day they were born. My friend and colleague, Gretchen Grinnell, once told me that little boys could be the gentlest and sweetest of creatures. And I didn't believe it–until my son was born. I have used my knowledge of feminism, of feminist theories, in raising him. And he is gentle and sweet, and he has paid some of the price for that, and I expect there is more to be paid later on. And I think of your son, how you have raised him with feminist principles and how he has put you through your paces, challenging you, often using your own words, about capitalism, patriarchy, life. I think of how the price these boy children have paid is to walk on the edge, teetering into the abyss, moving from the margins to the centre in often tenuous and tortuous ways. And we have walked there with them, often feeling scared, angry, enormously sad, and often weak. If our sons one day needed help from a clinic like ours, would we want that help to be there? The way we do it, with a feminist perspective, with the perspective you have articulated in your letter? Indeed I would.

So how do we traverse these boundaries? How do I accommodate my feelings of despair for men like we have described, juxtaposed on my feelings of outrage that we, as women, should be called upon, yet again, to Come To The Aid.

I think I traverse these borders by living as a double agent. One, by experiencing these men, in the moment, when they come to the clinic, when I'm with my son. Having compassion and sympathy and hope. As you do, I work to help these men and my son find those self-diversities, to embrace, accept, and live them. And then, in contrast, I experience my life, the totality of my life as a woman who is white and middle class, who doesn't have as many borders as you do, at least while I live in Canada, and who is conscious of the price women pay for being women, the price I have paid for being a woman.

Somewhere in that border crossing is where I live my contradictions.

Your friend,

Nikki

*   *   *

Dear Nikki,

Your reflections on our border-crossing struggles, which result in our living our contradictions at a personal level, provide a wonderful insight into what we go through in raising our sons according to feminist principles. Witnessing the pain in the lives of our sons, because of their resistance to a socially constructed male identity, often raises dilemmas for us that need resolutions. We do not have very many role models to look to in our search for their resolutions. The newness of this kind of work is a challenge but rewarding and worthy of pursuit.

One of its rewards is the emergence of subjectivity, which, as feminist therapists, we value very much. Its recognition and use in therapy often help us in connecting with the inner world of our clients. We see therapy as an engagement in reciprocal interactions between two human beings whose inner worlds are shaped by patriarchy and who need to border cross from the inner to the outer world, partly by naming and voicing feelings. Some male clients allow this engagement while others reject it. Those who accept it are often struggling to embrace the diversity of their "self"; those who don't have lost touch with this diversity–it is repressed, lost, long gone. The seduction of the rewards of a monolithic or what Jung (1968) calls "social persona" invokes intense fears in seeing one's self in any other way than "masculine." Their sense of self seems to be deeply immersed in the social norms and they feel that any attempt to change is doomed to failure. The presence of role models–sports heroes, tough corporate executives, military generals and other icons in the popular culture– is too tempting to be ignored.

One of my male clients fits this category. I find it exhausting to do the border crossing I need to while doing therapy with him. He frequently replays his male privilege in our sessions and guards any attempt of making connection with his inner world–his real feelings and beliefs or the repressed voices of those parts of self that frighten him.

For the protection of his confidentiality, I will call him Mr. L. Mr. L is thirty-five years old. He has been in several unsuccessful relationships with women and believes that "he attracts women who inherently lack appreciation for his sensitivity" and therefore, he needs help in getting rid of his attraction for such women. Mr. L has developed a physically disabling condition and is currently fighting for compensation on that ground. As well, one of his parents is dying. His life is not going very well and gives me reason to believe that he is feeling quite distressed. He acknowledges stress but attributes it to the callousness of his woman friend. Despite my efforts frequently to remind him of the contract of therapy, which is to provide support for his physical illness, he cannot stop himself from complaining about this woman. In fact, he has been charged for abusing her and has a history of being abusive to women.

Mr. L walks into the session with a smile on his face which contradicts the stiffness of his posture and lurking defensiveness in his eyes. The smile does not last very long. He shuts off all efforts at opening himself up.

I often use clay, music and narrative construction in therapy with clients. These techniques are often accepted by women while most men initially resist them but later start to accept them as useful tools for healing. Mr. L seems to have no use for them. I get the sense that men like him have some knowledge of or window on their self's diversity and the fear of this knowledge leads them to repress it. Mr. L values "toughness" and his definition of toughness is so embedded in patriarchy that he refuses any other perspective of toughness.

He presents himself as an innocent victim of his attraction to women who need fixing and these women as his victimizers. His non-stop narration of victimization discourages any interruptions–distractions that might destabilize him to the extent that he might disclose to himself the secret of his self's diversity.

Freyd (1997) conceptualizes a reaction of men who abuse women as the "Darvo Response" (p. 29). It stands for Denial, Attack and Reverse Victim Offender. Mr. L uses the Darvo Response to his own disadvantage. It makes him anxious and this augments his physical pain. Moreover, Darvo is a defensive mechanism and consumes his energy which he needs to explore and develop his self's diversity. If he would allow himself a better use of his energy he may be in less pain and may not need to fight fatal attractions. I have drawn his attention to his loss of those very valuable parts of self that could decrease his pain but he has refused the invitation to get in touch with those parts because he says he will lose "toughness women respect."

Sufis have written extensively on the pain of losing self's diversity. This pain, according to their writings, reflects itself in violent projection on others who are vulnerable and, in Mr. L's case, women.

Iqbal Mohammad, a Sufi poet of Pakistan, sees the repression of self's diversity as enslaving individuals and robbing them of "Khud-Agahi" or the knowledge and growth of self (Iqbal, 1965). The slavery experienced by men like Mr. L is a gift from a system that is created by men–patriarchy. Border crossing, which men need to do, means freedom to be and become who they really are meant to be. According to Jami, a Sufi philosopher, all human beings are essences and, "The essences are each a separate Glass, through which the sun of Being's Light is passed–Each tinted fragment sparkles in the Sun: A Thousand Colors, but the Light is One" (Shafi, 1985, p. 17). "Each tinted fragment" that is supposed to "sparkle" is buried deep in the darkness of repression. This darkness prevails on women and men because of patriarchy and as feminists we have to come to grips with this reality. Men need to do this work in order to create possibilities of freedom for us all.

This possibility seems possible when we discover societies that have escaped patriarchy. One such society exists in a remote northern region of Pakistan. It is known as Kalash society. Despite being surrounded by regions that are predominantly Muslim, the Kalash people have remained free from patriarchy. Though poor, they value peace and harmony, and worship a Goddess.

The vision of a world which women at the Fourth International Forum on Women, in Beijing in 1995, dreamt about is possible if the rest of the globe follows Kalash society, what Eurocentric discourse constructs as an "underdeveloped" region. Border crossing at the global level may mean stepping back into times when we did not have patriarchy, to dispel the myth that patriarchy and capitalism are inevitable–the fall of the Soviet bloc and globalization hysteria have reinforced this myth.

And so, Nikki, border crossing affects us at many different levels. Because we are feminists, we border cross the moment we take a breath in the morning. In our lives as feminists and in our work as feminist therapists, we will continue to be challenged by men and male clients. Let's hope that our contradictions sustain us.

Your friend,

Nayyar

REFERENCES

Arastch, A. (1965). *Romi the Persian: Rebirth in creativity and love.* Lahore, Pakistan: S. Ashraf.

Freyd, J. (1997). Violation of power, adaptive blindness and betrayal trauma theory. *Feminism and Psychology, 7*(1), 22-32.

hooks, b. (1994). *Outlaw culture: Resisting representations.* New York: Routledge.

Iqbal, M. (1965). *Bal-e-Jabriel.* Lahore, Pakistan: Sheikh Gulam Ali and Sons.

Jung, C. (1968). *Analytical psychology: Its theory and practice.* New York: Vintage.

Nurbacksh, J. (1983). *Sufi women.* New York: Khaniquhi-Nimatullahi Publications.

Romaniello, J. (1992). A feminist perspective on Jungian theory. In Brown, L.S. and Ballon, M. (Eds). *Personality and psychopathology: Feminist reappraisals.* New York: The Guilford Press.

Saul, J. (1995). *The unconscious civilization.* Toronto: House of Anansi Press Ltd.

Shafi, M. (1985). *Freedom from the self: Sufism, meditation and psychotherapy.* New York: Human Science Press.

Fostering Resistance
Through Relationships
in a Feminist Hospital Program

Renée Spencer

SUMMARY. This article is a discussion of the author's experience implementing a feminist hospital-based program for women. A description of the program is provided and the differences between a hospital program based on the theories of women's psychological development and a traditional psychiatric treatment program are highlighted. The application of relational theory and the feminist principles of the importance of context, the fostering of healthy resistance, and respect for clients' self-authority are each discussed and illustrated with clinical material. *[Article copies available for a fee from The Haworth Document Delivery Service: 1-800-342-9678. E-mail address: getinfo@haworth.com]*

Running a hospital-based feminist women's program was in many ways a political act. Although our program schedule looked similar to the other programs in the hospital, our practices were quite different. Bringing

---

Renée Spencer, MSSW, EdM, is a doctoral student in Human Development and Psychology at the Harvard University Graduate School of Education.

The author expresses special thanks to Alice Lawler and Sarah Shaw for their support and editorial suggestions.

Address correspondence to: Renée Spencer, 23 Stone Avenue, #3R, Somerville, MA 02143.

[Haworth co-indexing entry note]: "Fostering Resistance Through Relationships in a Feminist Hospital Program." Spencer, Renée. Co-published simultaneously in *Women & Therapy* (The Haworth Press, Inc.) Vol. 21, No. 2, 1998, pp. 101-111; and: *Feminist Therapy as a Political Act* (ed: Marcia Hill) The Haworth Press, Inc., 1998, pp. 101-111; and: *Feminist Therapy as a Political Act* (ed: Marcia Hill) The Harrington Park Press, an imprint of The Haworth Press, Inc., 1998, pp. 101-111. Single or multiple copies of this article are available for a fee from The Haworth Document Delivery Service [1-800-342-9678, 9:00 a.m. - 5:00 p.m. (EST). E-mail address: getinfo@haworth.com].

© 1998 by The Haworth Press, Inc. All rights reserved.

101

the principles of feminist therapy into a hospital setting was quite challenging. Common practices had to be re-thought and our language and attitudes—about the women, ourselves, and our relationships with them—had to be changed. I discovered that the more we moved away from the traditional medical model practices, the more the women who participated in the program challenged us to move even further.

The differences between this women's program and more traditional psychiatric hospital programs reflect four major shifts in thinking based on principles outlined in the literature on the psychology of women and feminist therapy. (1) Our theoretical base was the relational approach, put forth by the women of the Stone Center, which views both psychological distress and harm, and psychological health and healing, as arising within the context of relationships (Miller, 1988; Miller & Fidele, 1988; Miller & Stiver, 1991). (2) We recognized that a woman's psychological distress can only be fully understood when it is located within her relational and sociocultural contexts (Brown, 1994; Miller, 1988). (3) Fostering resistance was placed at the center of treatment (Brown, 1994; Gilligan, 1990). (4) We saw the women as the experts on their own lives and their treatment (Brown, 1994).

THE PROGRAM

This women's program was a partial hospital evening program offered by a private for-profit psychiatric hospital. It was uniquely supported by the local therapeutic community in that a committee comprised of feminist independent psychotherapy practitioners met regularly and acted as consultants. Typically, the women who were admitted to the program were presenting with difficulties with major depression, post-traumatic stress disorders, eating disorders, and anxiety disorders. Their symptoms were such that they were having significant difficulty functioning. Many were unable to go to work or take care of their family responsibilities. Some had suicidal ideation. Most of the women who attended this program were white and middle class. A few women of color, primarily Hispanic and African-American women, participated. The hospital allowed us to offer free care to about 25% of the women we served. We were not, however, able to offer regular transportation or child-care, which thereby limited access to the program for many women.

The program was intended to provide intensive treatment to women who needed more than outpatient psychotherapy but who did not need 24-hour care. Some women came directly into the program while others were transitioning from an inpatient stay. Lengths of stay ranged from 1 week to 8 weeks. Most of the women attended for 3-4 weeks. The primary treatment modality was group therapy. Women who were in individual psychotherapy were encouraged to continue working with their primary therapists while in the program. For those women who did not yet have an outpatient therapist, we gave them referrals and, if necessary, provided individual therapy until they connected with their new therapist. Individual nutritional counseling was regularly provided for all of the women with eating disorders and on an as-needed basis for the other women.

The women attended the program Monday-Thursday for four hours in the evening and then met for one short group on Fridays. The evening began with a brief "check-in" group in which each of the women talked about how things had gone for them that day and identified something they would like to focus on while in the program that evening. We then, as a group, had dinner together in the hospital cafeteria. After dinner, I facilitated a therapy group, which was followed by what we called a skill building group, facilitated by the program nurse. We concluded the evening with a wrap-up group which included a brief meditation.

THE THEORETICAL BASE

The central theoretical framework for the program was relational theory as developed by Jean Baker Miller and her colleagues at the Stone Center. In this view, psychological development occurs in and through increasingly complex relationships. Psychological health is the outgrowth of connection with others while psychological distress develops in response to repeated and chronic patterns of disconnection (Jordan, 1989; Miller, 1988; Miller & Stiver, 1994; Miller & Stiver, 1995).

Miller (1988) states that what we have called psychopathology occurs as a result of chronic patterns of disconnection without re-connection. When attempts to change the interaction or to move out of disconnection and into connection fail, the focus then shifts towards changing the self or controlling one's emotional responses. A problem of relationship becomes experienced as a problem of the self. Where the most chronic and/or severe forms of disconnection occur, the person becomes locked in what Miller calls a state of "condemned isolation." That is, the person then feels "locked out of the possibility of human connection" (Miller, 1988, p. 7). It was in this state of "condemned isolation" and powerlessness that the women came to the program. Many feared they were crazy, or broken and simply beyond repair.

Frequently, I would put up on the dry-erase board the five outcomes of connection and the five outcomes of disconnection as identified by Miller

(1988). The group would then discuss their reactions to these ideas and talk about their own relational experiences. The outcomes of disconnection were much more familiar to many of the women. Many could identify at least one relationship in which they had experienced connection. Some could not. A few stated they had never had this experience with another person, only with a pet.

This shift of focus away from individual pathology or "brokeness," to looking at their experiences within the context of their primary relationships, helped the women to see that their symptoms were not signs that they were sick or crazy, but rather the consequences of repeated and chronic disconnection in relationships. Often, as a woman talked about what her relationships had been like and were like currently, other group members would begin to feel and express empathy towards her. They would say things to one another like, "Well, it's no wonder you feel so depressed." When a woman spoke about feeling connected in her relationships, we would talk about what it was about that relationship that facilitated that connection, how she felt about the other person, their relationship, and how she experienced herself in the context of that connected relationship. We also discussed the ways in which the women felt connection and disconnection in the group and in the program as a whole.

In this model, healing occurs in the context of connected relationships. Therefore, building connections among us was central to the program. We attempted to foster connections in many ways. The women were not discouraged from having contact with one another outside of the group. Some of the women provided one another with quite a bit of daily support. A few built friendships. When problems did arise, we became facilitators and assisted the women in trying to work things out.

The evening meal became an important time for developing connections between the women in the program and the staff. We all ate together in the hospital cafeteria–the women in the program, the nurse, any student interns who were working with us at the time, and myself. Dinner was a social time. We engaged in small talk, gossiped, told stories, and laughed. I had the opportunity to hear the women talk about the many different facets of their lives. I heard about their children, their partners, and their pets. They talked about their current jobs and past careers. They shared their dream vacation or what they would do if they won the lottery. This more casual setting, of course, meant that I shared some of these parts of myself with them as well.

The therapy and skill-building groups provided numerous opportunities for fostering connections and working through disconnections. The women talked about the benefit of simply having the opportunity to listen to other women share their thoughts, feelings, and experiences. Many had never been in a group with only women and said that in this context they felt more able to talk about things that they had previously felt too ashamed about to share with anyone. Once they had felt the validation of the other group members, some were able to begin to share these parts of themselves with other people in their lives.

There were also many moments of disconnection. At one point, the hospital was laying off employees and the tension in the hallways was palpable. The women were furious about the layoffs, and the subsequent chaos in the hospital, and the therapy group that night was filled with criticisms of me, the program, and the hospital as a whole. I responded first, as I often did, by addressing the complaints at face value. Nothing seemed to have an effect. I felt myself trapped in what Miller and Stiver (1995) call a relational image. I felt like an inadequate caregiver and authority figure. I expressed my frustration and shared with the women that I was beginning to feel like a school principal. I asked them each to think about and tell the group the "lens" (a concrete way of talking about relational images) through which they might be seeing me and the hospital and how they were experiencing themselves in relation to these images.

Their responses were rich and different. One woman was feeling how she felt with her child's caseworker and felt afraid of my power to take something away from her. Another felt like a child herself and said that if she did not make demands she feared that she would simply be ignored as she was in her family during times of conflict. Some felt responsible as did one woman who somehow felt that she had caused the chaos by being a "bad patient." This process brought us back into connection and the women began talking more directly about what it was like for them to be surrounded by the chaos and tension at the hospital. We were then able to discuss what we could do to insure that they did get their needs met during this difficult time.

WOMEN'S PSYCHOLOGICAL DISTRESS IN CONTEXT

The theoretical base of the hospital within which the women's program existed was cognitive. We did incorporate many of these techniques, but re-framed them from a relational perspective. Rather than "cognitive distortions" or "irrational thoughts," we talked about "distressing cognition" or thoughts that contributed to feelings of distress. When eliciting and looking at automatic thoughts, we talked about where these thoughts came from, what the context was in which they developed, and the contexts in which they were currently arising. The women noticed patterns among each others' negative cognition and began questioning why it was that they were experiencing similar kinds of distress.

Most of the women were struggling with depression, eating disorders, and post-traumatic stress disorders. We talked about the gender difference in prevalence rates of depression, discussed victimization rates of women, and the objectification of women and the disconnection of women from their bodies. We then examined the particular relational and cultural contexts in which they developed their beliefs about themselves.

Locating the women within their own particular relational and sociocultural contexts was essential to building therapeutic relationships. In hospitals, patients are thought of mainly in terms of their pathology, which is isolated and meticulously described. The emphasis on pathology has contributed to a great divide between patient and therapist. The line of demarcation has been health–the assumption being that the psychologically healthy therapist is to heal the psychologically sick patient. Much emphasis in training is placed on observing and naming particular sicknesses and developing and implementing treatments or cures.

Headway has certainly been made in feminist circles to address this split. In hospitals, however, this can be particularly challenging. Only some people have keys and are not locked in or out. Only some have free access to information and write in the medical records, know and enforce the rules and determine what is appropriate and inappropriate behavior, and hold legitimate power within the system. We ostensibly hold this power because we are well, and claim the authority to hold this power over others because they are sick. This divide, and the assumptions that accompany it, are unquestioned in a hospital setting.

When I found myself thinking about the women or their symptoms in isolation, the divide grew larger. When I worked with the women to place themselves within a larger context, to understand them and their symptoms within particular relational (personal, social, and cultural) contexts, the divide became smaller. When I spoke about the women or wrote in their charts, I always kept in my mind an awareness of whether or not I thought they would see themselves in my words. Was I capturing their experience? I thought about my own psychological struggles and how they might be represented by a mental health professional in a hospital chart. I speculated about what my diagnoses would be and how my progress notes would read.

FOSTERING RESISTANCE

Laura Brown, in her aptly titled book *Subversive Dialogues,* writes, "Central to a feminist theory of psychotherapy is the idea that the models of personal change must promote resistance" (Brown, 1994, p. 24). We viewed the symptoms the women were experiencing as signs of psychological distress and therefore, in part, as signs of unconscious resistance. We worked with the women to foster more conscious forms of resistance which did not involve self-harm.

Psychological symptoms can be what Gilligan, in her work with adolescent girls, has called "psychological resistance"–"a reluctance to know what one knows and a fear that such knowledge, if spoken, will endanger relationships and threaten survival" (Gilligan, 1990, p. 502). In Gilligan's view, when girls' conflicts of self and relationship are pushed underground, psychological resistance sets in. Adopting this framework, we worked with the women to shift this psychological resistance to what Gilligan has called "political resistance" or "an insistence to know what one knows and a willingness to be outspoken" (Gilligan, 1990, p. 502). As we worked with the women to both manage and contextualize their psychological symptoms, the conflicts between self and relationship, and self and sociocultural context, began to re-surface. The women's program provided a forum to wrestle with these conflicts in the presence of the support of other women and opportunities to speak out about things which had previously been unspoken.

The women entered the program experiencing high levels of psychological distress which impeded their functioning on a daily basis. They were unable to sleep well, think clearly, eat or stop eating. They were having panic attacks or flashbacks and nightmares. Some were obsessed with cutting on themselves or killing themselves. Our first priority was to work with the women to manage or relieve these debilitating symptoms and to help them improve their functioning levels as quickly as possible. Drawing from the trauma model of recovery, establishing or re-establishing safety and restoring control became a critical component of the treatment (Herman, 1992).

We began by sharing our knowledge with the women and de-mystifying psychiatric treatment. Many of the skill-building groups focused on the different diagnoses the women had been given by their physicians, what the criteria were, which medications are typically prescribed, why, and what they do and how they work. We also taught basic stress-management techniques and discussed topics such as self-esteem and body image.

The purpose of these groups was not simply to impart information. We contextualized these issues. In a group on depression, we discussed the high rate of depression in women. In groups about body image, the socio-cultural context in which women develop their body image was discussed. Self-esteem was not presented as the first and foremost step on the road to healthy relationships, but rather, we talked about it as an outgrowth of healthy relationships. We encouraged the women to identify their strengths and talked about how they may value qualities in themselves that are devalued by the culture.

As a group, we brainstormed strategies for symptom management for each of the women. The women realized that they had wonderful ideas for one another, chipping away at their sense of helplessness. We were encouraged by signs of action or activity–when the women no longer internalized their distress but began to identify the real challenges in their lives and began to think actively about how they wanted to approach them. We were also encouraged when the women became more connected with their strengths and realized that there were things about themselves and about their lives that they did not want to change.

Sometimes the women chose what on the surface might have appeared to be inaction. Many decided to stay in difficult marriages that were clearly contributing to their depression. Leaving posed greater conflicts for them. These conscious choices, while they did not change the actual situation the woman was in, did allow her, then, to more directly think about what she might need to take care of herself psychologically.

WOMEN AS EXPERTS

Each week, the women met with their psychiatrist and the program staff for a weekly treatment plan review. Rather than having the treatment team present our assessments of their progress and give them our recommendations, we talked together with the women about their experiences in the program. We began by asking what they wanted to discuss in the meeting. We talked about how they were doing, if they were aware of any progress, and how the program and their particular course of treatment were going. We talked about what was working, what was not, and how long they thought they needed to be in the program.

Adhering to this belief in women as authorities over their own lives created difficult dilemmas. We came upon moments when what we thought was best for a particular woman and what she thought was right for her were at odds. One woman came to the program with severe anorexia. Her body fat was less than 10% and her lab results looked bad. Due to her particular family history, which had involved negative experiences with psychiatric hospitals, she steadfastly refused inpatient care. We agreed to work with her through the women's program.

She made slow but promising gains in her first 2 weeks in the program. Then, she told us about a dream vacation she and her husband had been planning for over a year, stating that she would be gone for a week. All of the members of the treatment team agreed that this was simply too risky. She thanked us for our concern and stated that she was going anyway. She also talked about how important this trip was to her and why she felt she simply had to go.

We were at an impasse. We could make our recommendation that she stay and inform her that, should she go anyway, we would then discharge her from the program AMA–"against medical advice." In essence, we could threaten her with refusing to work with her. We were also concerned about her insurance reviewer and whether or not the insurance company would refuse to continue paying for treatment if she left for a week. We decided instead to appraise her of the risks to her health, inform her of the possibility that her insurance company would deny further treatment, and re-stated our recommendation that she not go. We also told her what we would do to support her if she decided to take the trip anyway. She did go, armed with an explicit plan for meals and care for her health, and came back to the program a week later.

We were often faced with the constraints of working within a system dominated by managed care. We advocated for the women and also supported them in advocating for themselves. We learned to speak openly and honestly about the limits of the health care system and of the hospital itself. Some women asked to speak to their insurance reviewers and to read their charts. We talked about their frustration, anger, and disappointment when they were not able to get what they, and we, knew they needed. We strategized, not about how to learn not to have needs, but about where else they could go to get their needs met.

Finally, we took the complaints, criticisms and suggestions made by the women in the program seriously. Fresh out of graduate school, I began working as a therapist in a psychiatric hospital. I can still remember my outrage as I repeatedly heard patients' legitimate complaints about the hospital dismissed outright as resistance to treatment. I felt ashamed of my desire to join with the patients as it was clear that my response would also be interpreted by my colleagues—most likely as naivete. Privately I did join with the patients, either individually or when I was running a group by myself. As my authority grew within the hospital system, so did my courage. By the time I had the opportunity to design and open the women's program, I had learned that some of the best ideas for how to run a successful hospital program were going to come from the real experts of the program: the women themselves.

CLOSING REFLECTIONS

I found both the support for, and the resistance to, a women's program to be strong. Many of the nurses, therapists, physicians, clinicians on the assessment team and the clients saw the need for and the benefits of this type of program immediately. The responses were "it's about time," "I have been looking for a program like this and have wondered why it has not been out there," "it makes so much sense," and from many of the female hospital employees, "can I be in the program?" Resistance to the program included, "I do not want to send patients to a program that will encourage them to bust up their families," "I do not want the patient in those groups getting all stirred up and falling apart," "If she goes in that program, she will become too dependent and we will never get her out." These responses sounded to me like that old familiar refrain about the bottomless pit of women's needs and the intense fear of what might happen if women got together and began to talk.

The program did operate within a patriarchal system which reflected the larger patriarchal culture. I often felt overwhelmed by the roadblocks and barriers, and struggled with my own complicity with the system by running this program. I felt the dilemmas renewed as I wrote this paper. I found myself using language like "treatment" that does not quite fit and being aware that this was the language I used while running the program. Writing about the women who participated made me aware, again, of the limited and privileged group of women that we served–mostly white middle-class women. I remembered how the survival of the program was always in question. It was the program most often named as number one on the chopping block, despite the fact that it was profitable, and how that had the awful effect of making me feel grateful for being "allowed" to run it. I see now that I allowed that atmosphere to hold me back from being more forceful in my insistence about what practices simply had to be changed.

However, I took heart then, and still do now, in the changes we were able to make and the bridges we did begin to build. Bringing relational theory and feminist practices into a hospital setting was truly a political act. We had the opportunity to offer a different type of mental health service and to foster political resistance in the women who came to this program. We created a safer place for women to get support during a time of psychological crises by taking risks to do things differently and it worked. I hope that my experiences will spark others to take action that continues to move hospital programs many steps further toward subversion.

REFERENCES

Brown, L. S. (1994). *Subversive dialogues: Theory in feminist therapy.* New York: Basic Books.

Gilligan, C. (1990). Joining the resistance: Psychology, politics, girls and women. *Michigan Quarterly Review, 29* (4), 501-536.

Herman, J. L. (1992). *Trauma and recovery.* New York: Basic Books.

Jordan, J. V. (1989). Relational development: Therapeutic implications of empathy and shame. *Work in Progress, # 39.* Wellesley, MA: Stone Center Working Papers Series.

Miller, J. B. (1988). Connections, disconnection and violations. *Work in Progress, # 33.* Wellesley, MA: Stone Center Working Papers Series.

Miller, J. B. & Fidele, N. F. (1988). Putting theory into practice: Creating mental health programs for women. *Work in Progress, #32.* Wellesley, MA: Stone Center Working Papers Series.

Miller, J. B. & Stiver, I. P. (1991). A relational reframing of therapy. *Work in Progress, #52.* Wellesley, MA: Stone Center Working Papers Series.

Miller, J. B. & Stiver, I. P. (1994). Movement in therapy: Honoring the "strategies of disconnection." *Work in Progress, #65.* Wellesley, MA: Stone Center Working Papers Series.

Miller, J. B. & Stiver, I. P. (1995). Relational images and their meanings in psychotherapy. *Work in Progress, #74.* Wellesley, MA: Stone Center Working Papers Series.

Tools for Change:
Methods of Incorporating
Political/Social Action
into the Therapy Session

Kayla Miriyam Weiner

SUMMARY. This paper discusses the ways in which one may incorporate political action into a client's therapy process so the client may incorporate it into her/his life. A framework for defining this as ethical, therapeutic and necessary to the client is presented. A number of suggestions for helping clients and therapists to become more politically active, as well as vignettes demonstrating how this might work with clients in the therapy process are provided. *[Article copies available for a fee from The Haworth Document Delivery Service: 1-800-342-9678. E-mail address: getinfo@haworth.com]*

It is not required that you complete the task, but neither are you free to desist from it.

--Pirke Avot

Kayla Miriyam Weiner, PhD, is a feminist/psychodynamic/existential psychotherapist in independent practice in Seattle, WA. She specializes in working with people who have experienced trauma in their lives, or are in the midst of a life transition, or are addressing Jewish or adoption issues. When not practicing Tikkun Olam (repairing the world), her greatest pleasures include travel, gardening and spending time with friends.

Address correspondence to: Kayla Weiner, PhD, Pioneer Building, 600 First Avenue, Suite 530, Seattle, WA 98104 (E-mail: kayla-weiner@worldnet.att.net).

[Haworth co-indexing entry note]: "Tools for Change: Methods of Incorporating Political/Social Action into the Therapy Session." Weiner, Kayla Miriyam. Co-published simultaneously in *Women & Therapy* (The Haworth Press, Inc.) Vol. 21, No. 2, 1998, pp. 113-123; and: *Feminist Therapy as a Political Act* (ed: Marcia Hill) The Haworth Press, Inc., 1998, pp. 113-123; and: *Feminist Therapy as a Political Act* (ed: Marcia Hill) The Harrington Park Press, an imprint of The Haworth Press, Inc., 1998, pp. 113-123. Single or multiple copies of this article are available for a fee from The Haworth Document Delivery Service [1-800-342-9678, 9:00 a.m. - 5:00 p.m. (EST). E-mail address: getinfo@haworth.com].

© 1998 by The Haworth Press, Inc. All rights reserved.

Anything someone does to improve the lives of others, individually or collectively, or does to make the world a better place for all people is, by my definition, a form of political action. The words political action and social action are used interchangeably in this paper. This action could be anything from writing letters to congresspeople about an affirmative action program, to supporting an anti-discrimination bill, to keeping one's children in a public school while working to improve the schools, to volunteering at a church, hospice or child care center. Each individual must choose her/his own path of action, one that is congruent with who s/he is and how s/he works in the world. The criterion is not how radical the action, but rather that the world is a better place for what has been done.

Each of the three philosophical systems that I draw on to define myself, Judaism, feminism and feminist psychology, has taught me that political action is not an option in life but rather a requirement. An ancient Jewish Babylonian Talmudic (Talmud is an explanation of the Old Testament) saying states: "Tzedakah is as important as all the other commandments together." Tzedakah is a way of giving to individuals and the world, and Judaism describes many levels of giving. Jews are charged to feed the hungry, clothe the poor, house the homeless and heal the wounded. There are commandments as specific as "one should not put a stumbling block in front of the blind." Another instructs that if one is to take a poor person's coat as collateral for a loan, one must return it every night so the person is protected from the cold. This metaphor, in part, means that one is never to injure another. Within the framework of Tzedakah, Tikkun Olam is the injunction to repair the world. Tikkun Olam requires anyone who considers herself or himself righteous to work constantly to make the world a better place for all people.

Two pithy sayings of the feminist movement that emerged from the civil rights movement of the 1960s, "The personal is political" (Hanisch, 1970), and "You're either part of the solution or part of the problem" attributed to Eldridge Cleaver, reverberate within me and resonate with my already deeply held views of social action. It seems important to elaborate on the meaning of these two statements. It is not adequate just to understand oppression as an idea, and for instance, to support the concept of personal empowerment and be willing to write or talk about the theories. It is necessary to realize that what one does in one's life, every minute of every day, has political implications. If one is driving a car one is driving on tires that were made by exploiting an impoverished country. One may not be able to avoid that reality, but it is important that one is conscious of the fact and works to mitigate exploitation in the world. If one buys clothes and doesn't know where they were produced, one may very well be contributing to the exploitation of children forced to work in sweatshops. If one lives in a segregated neighborhood, one is contributing, de facto, to the classism and racism that permeates our society. If one doesn't vote, it has an implication. If one does vote, it has an implication. Where one takes a vacation has an implication. Each individual must realize that every action they take or don't take has a ripple effect and makes a political statement in a positive or negative way. One need not be paralyzed by this realization, but one must be mindful and very conscious about each and every action one chooses to take or not take.

The second statement, "You are part of the solution or you are part of the problem," intensifies the first statement because it says that whatever you choose to do must be done from a position of consciousness and intent because your action, if it is not a means of making the world better, then absolutely makes the world worse. There is no neutrality. Not doing something is acceptable if it will make the world better (i.e., not making racist statements) and doing something is fine (i.e., picketing a company with homophobic policies), but every action or non-action has a political implication and one must be constantly diligent about being sure one is part of the solution. At a concert in Seattle in the 1980s I heard folk singer/social activist Holly Near say that "political/social action is the dues you pay for living on the planet." She went on to say that a commitment to work to eliminate oppression for all people is something one must do one's entire life; it is not a time limited obligation.

Feminist theory recognizes the impact that society has on the individual, through sexism and other forms of oppression, which create and maintain the problems and issues brought into therapy (Feminist Therapy Institute, 1987). The preamble of the *Feminist Therapy Code of Ethics* (1987) states,

> Basic tenets of feminism include a belief in the equal worth of all human beings, a recognition that each individual's personal experiences and situations are reflective of, and influence on, society's institutionalized attitudes and values, and a commitment to political and social change that equalizes power among people.

The ethical guidelines state, "A feminist therapist seeks multiple avenues for impacting (sic) change. . . . " It follows, therefore, that each client must be provided with the basic tenets of feminist philosophy and political theory. Incorporating an understanding of political and social action into the therapy process is a responsibility of the feminist therapist. The healing of the individual is only the first step in a process to enable one to join in the healing of the society/environment. When a client has released the pains of the past s/he usually begins to ask the existential questions of the meaning of her/his life experiences and her/his purpose on the planet in the future. It is at this point in the therapy process when a client is most ready to begin being a part of the solution to the problems of the world (although the ideas may be presented throughout the healing process).

Thus it is a therapist's obligation to educate her/his client about social responsibility. However, the therapist is not free to push a client into any specific form of action or thinking. Rather, the therapeutic process requires that the client learn about her/his relationship to the world and her/his duty to define her/his own direction in political/social action. It is the therapist's role to bring a larger political/social framework into the therapy context and allow the client to guide her/his own path.

POLITICAL ACTION IN THE THERAPY SETTING

Miriam Greenspan (1983) notes that during her residency a woman was chastised for not wearing a bra because she "made a personal statement to the patient" according to her male instructor. Of course, Greenspan noted, it never occurred to him that his suit and tie also made a very strong personal statement to the client. Everything we have in our office makes a personal/political statement. If one is in a small, cramped, uncomfortable office it makes a statement and if one is in an expensive, large, lavishly furnished office it makes a statement to a client. The art work we have makes a statement. Are the items all representative of white, heterosexual, able-bodied cultures? Do you have dolls of color or art from other countries? The kind of clothes we wear, how we comb our hair and how we sit in a chair all say something to a client.

The *Feminist Therapy Code of Ethics* (1987) states: "A feminist therapist discloses information to the client which facilitates the therapeutic process." I believe it is ethical and therapeutic to be direct and open with clients concerning one's own sense of responsibility to the world so the client will not be confused or be forced to make assumptions about the therapist's position. Leaving the client to create her/his own fantasies can do more harm than good. If the therapist is publicly well known, it is virtually impossible to be anonymous, so to be forthright is much more beneficial for the therapeutic process. The client need not conjecture about the therapist and can spend her/his energy on her/his own therapy process. This type of disclosure does not include matters personal to the therapist which most definitely do not belong in the therapy room (Feminist Therapy Institute, 1987).

Although the following examples may not be feasible in all therapeutic settings, they are examples of how some therapists have applied the principle of social action within their practices. Each therapist must find the actions that are right for her/him by modifying those suggested and adding new ones.

One method that is very useful for helping clients to begin to see themselves as a part of the world, in it and responsible for it, is to have a bulletin board in the waiting area of your office. A bulletin board can serve many functions for the therapy process. It can be a place for sharing of information of general interest. It can be used to demonstrate a variety of ways that people are involved in the world. It can display a wide variety of perspectives and ideas. It is a form of consciousness raising. A quick perusal of one therapist's bulletin board included the following: several pithy sayings, including Alice Walker's definition of womanist, to provide some intellectual stimulation. A political cartoon from the Religious Coalition for Abortion Rights to present the issue of personal choice and open the possibility for consideration for women with religious concerns. A brochure discussing insurance quandaries and questions to help clients get some understanding about how managed care and insurance companies are affecting them. An article about Ang San Sui Kyi, the Burmese freedom fighter, to present the universality of women's activism. A call from a Police Department for volunteers to help in a program for battered women. A copy of the newsletter *One Voice,* which is about abuse, to help some women to understand they are not alone. A poem entitled, "a poem for men who don't understand when we say they have it" to introduce the concept of gender privilege. A schedule for courses in self-defense training to encourage the idea of self-protection. A flyer from a local fat women's advocacy group. There are newspapers put out by numerous women's studies programs, as well as newspapers from the National Women's Health Network, a local homeless advocacy group, the National Organization for Women, the Feminist Women's Health Center (a local abortion clinic), The Children's Alliance, and a Spiritual Healing Center, all as a means of exposing clients to possibilities in the world for them and others. There is a poster for the local AIDS walk and condoms (male and female) in a bowl nearby. There are pink ribbons in a bowl as a means to demonstrate support for breast cancer awareness, and an announcement for a lesbian breast cancer study. There is environmental information, brochures for the Adoption Resource Center that sponsors activities for all parties in the adoption/birth triad, an announcement of workshops for those involved in divorce from a local organization called Divorce Lifeline and one from a local mediator who specializes in amicable endings.

Updates of community action such as Take Back the Night marches, the Martin Luther King March, and new programs and items of interest are added regularly. The variety of items posted on the board provide something of interest to each person as well as introducing everyone to something they may never have previously considered. In addition, magazines in this office are all chosen with political/social action in mind. There is usually a selection of *MS magazine, On the Issues, Lilith* (a Jewish feminist magazine), *National Wildlife,* and *The Funny Times* (a political newspaper done entirely with cartoon and humor), all intended to educate and raise consciousness.

In one office a pure water dispenser in the waiting area of one therapist is available to clients, but there are no paper or plastic cups. Each client has her/his own mug and is responsible for keeping it sanitary and is educated that the mugs are an environmental protection action, intended to preserve nonrenewable resources by not using paper and not filling the landfills with non-biodegradable styrofoam.

A therapist might find ways to make it obvious that her/his office is in a building that has a recycling system or that the therapist has arranged for recycling. The importance of being in an office that is wheelchair accessible could be noted. Political/social matters can be pointed out during the course of therapy in numerous ways including, but not limited to, the disclosure statement, the above mentioned bulletin board or in discussion with the client. These points are not to be made as a "mantra" but more as a matter of course, to help clients become more aware of the interrelationship of all things in life and the individual's connection to them.

Throughout a person's time in therapy, the clinician can ask, repeatedly, three important questions when clients raise issues. The first question is, "Who does it benefit?" followed by, "Who does it hurt?" and finally, "What can you do about it?" These questions will keep the client focused on the systemic, rather than the individual causes of problems in the world. Discussions can lead to helping clients discover ways in which they might make a difference in their own lives and in the lives of others.

By assisting clients to realize that there are small things we can control in our environment, we can lead them to realize there are larger things over which they have control. It is useful to insert frequently into discussions examples of "outrageous acts and everyday rebellions" (Steinem, 1983) and help the clients devise their own methods of taking action in the world. As an example, I tell of the time I heard a commercial on the radio that was very offensive in the way it depicted Native Americans. I called the station and the person explained that the commercial came over the wire and had not been reviewed. As soon as I called their attention to the offensiveness, the commercial was removed from the air. Clients may be encouraged to write letters to companies, businesses, or congresspeople when they are concerned about an issue. Learning the importance of sending a thank you note to someone who has done something healing for the world is also an "outrageous act" that makes a difference and may be presented as part of the therapy process. When clients are talking about buying books they may be encouraged to support local bookstores by explaining how large bookstore conglomerates are running small bookstores and small publishers out of business. Clients may be helped to see that supporting locally owned businesses increases the viability of their own neighborhood and improves the lives of others. These are small acts, which most people can do if they are provided with the education, support and encouragement, that help the world and enhance the self-esteem of the person who has taken the action.

When clients are concerned about their child-rearing practices and the values they want their children to hold, they may be helped to find an activity that involves the entire family as well as contributes to the world. An example may be presented of someone who takes her/his children to the food bank every other week and delivers food to homebound people, many of whom are immigrants and elderly, to provide inspiration. These children not only have the experience of doing a good deed, but they get to meet a variety of people they might not have met otherwise. Another example is a family who goes monthly to serve dinner to homeless youth at a local shelter. These are examples of activities that are shared by parents and children that improve the world and provide excellent models for the children.

Fear of being visible and therefore in possible danger, and the fear of being singled out by others as "not nice," often keeps people from taking actions that they would otherwise like to take. It is therefore important for the therapist to be proactive and intentional in being a role model for her/his clients. When a client raises a social issue that concerns her/him, a therapist may note when s/he is going/has gone to a demonstration or fund-raising activity related to that particular subject. In so doing s/he brings this type of action into the consciousness of the client as something that is possible for the client. This is an excellent opportunity to address how joining with others makes political action much more safe (as well as much more fun). It is a way to emphasize the collective solution to the collective problem.

Each of us has within her life examples of "outrageous acts and everyday rebellions" and these can be shared with clients when they are related to, and specific to, the client's situation. In addition, the therapist can listen to and learn from clients when they share their ways to improve the world. A feminist therapist understands the power dynamic inherent in the therapeutic relationship and understands she cannot avoid influencing a client. However, she models the effective use of power and uses the power differential to the benefit of the client, never taking control that rightfully belongs to the client (Feminist Therapy Institute, 1987). The therapeutic health of the client is the overarching criterion on which all other decisions are made. One only introduces into any session that which is to the therapeutic benefit of the client at a particular time.

Vignette of an Appropriate *Political Intervention into the Therapy Process*

A woman was present when a co-worker, a friend of hers for over 15 years, stole an expensive item from the company. She worried for weeks about what to do about the situation. Her therapist helped her examine what her beliefs were about honesty, what she wanted to do in her heart, and why she was afraid to tell her employer. One of her fears was "making someone angry and having them not like me" and another was the fear of losing her own job for not coming forward immediately. During the period of time she was discussing this with her therapist and she was coming to a conclusion of what she wanted to do, she found herself blurting out the truth to her manager during lunch one day. She felt immediately relieved to have told the truth, but frightened about her job. She went to the human resource person to get some kind of confirmation that her job was safe but could get no reassurance. About a week after the disclosure and several days after the other person was fired, the woman received a note from management stating that she was being written up for not coming forward sooner. The woman was very hurt. "After all," she said, "if I hadn't told, they never would have gotten the material back and they would still have a thief working here." After talking about the situation in therapy, the therapist suggested the client might want to write a letter to the regional manager who had sent the reprimand. She wrote the letter at home, and reviewed it in session with her therapist to be sure it said what she wanted it to say in a constructive manner. Her letter stated what had happened, how she felt about it and asked that the reprimand be removed from her file but if that was not possible, that at least her detailed letter of the events and circumstances be added to her file. And she asked for an apology. To her surprise, and adding to her sense of empowerment, the regional manager traveled to her city to meet with her and explain the situation ("policy") and indeed did thank her. Her job is also secure. This action, which seems to be personal on the surface, is actually an important social action. She not only learned that she had some power over her own life, but she found she could make a difference. She is beginning now to look for volunteer work to add meaning to her life. Her therapeutic work is now to find a direction for herself. Because she is a battered woman she is looking into working with other battered women. In this way she can feel herself competent and she can experience the joy of being in unity with other women.

If she cannot find a place to work in that capacity, her other focus of interest is her church as a source of volunteer opportunities. Over the years her church, a very fundamentalist sect, has brought her pain and confusion. She has worked to define her own belief system without having to throw away her connection with the church. Therefore, she has that community, and her work will be congruent with who she is as a person. Any work one does to improve the lives of others, no matter what the venue, improves the world. Any improvement in the world sphere, improves the lives of individuals.

Vignette of an Inappropriate *Political Intervention into the Therapy Process*

A therapist had been seeing a client for about five years. This young woman had been seriously traumatized by the adults in her life. In spite of that, this woman is astonishingly insightful and is completely aware of the interrelationships of the various oppressions and is herself very politically active. One of the most difficult problems the client has had has been her inability to accept herself for her profound talents and to believe that she is a very gifted leader. She had taken almost ten years to complete her bachelor's degree and had proceeded to take numerous entry level jobs for minimal pay and no status. After a time she was offered a research position at a local institute that is rather anonymous to most people. She moved into the position, and began to appreciate her skills and experience her own talents as mirrored by others of high regard.

It just so happened that the therapist was aware that this company has been involved in weapons development. The therapist knows the client would be appalled to learn this but the therapist is aware that it is not in the client's therapeutic interest to learn of these things at this time. She must be allowed to benefit fully from her experience and learn about the "underside" of the company in her own time. Inserting political information into the process at this time would prioritize the therapist's agenda over the needs of the client.

Vignette of an Appropriate Political Intervention into the Therapy Process

A woman who had been sexually abused as a child told her therapist about how terrified she became when people touched her, especially when the person was a stranger. She did not know how to keep it from happening and was concerned about how it would affect her life if she didn't take control of her body. The therapist recalled an incident in which she was in a restaurant and the waitperson, a man, came to the table and put a hand on the shoulder of each of the two women on each side of him. The therapist explained how she had spoken to the waiter explaining to him that many people do not like to be touched without first being asked permission. The therapist went on to explain to the man that many abused people are severely traumatized when people touch them and often can't say anything to stop it, therefore the waitperson would do well not to touch people in his restaurant. This example provided the client with a possible method of handling the situation for herself as well as an example of how things done for oneself can have a larger impact. In this case the waitperson will probably not put his hands on other women who may be traumatized by the experience.

CONCLUSION

It is useful to reiterate the purposes for incorporating political/social action into the therapy process. They are: (1) to provide a client with a political/social context for her/his pain and healing, (2) to strengthen the client's sense of power in the world, (3) to help the client enlarge her/his sense of personal identity, (4) to complete healing by joining with others in social action, and (5) to make the world a better place for all people.

The process of therapy is, in a sense, the process of pushing boundaries. That is, the client is helped and guided to push herself/himself beyond her/his previous limits in order to define one's self more clearly, as well as to find one's self in the world. As has been noted throughout this paper, even what may appear to be a small act of "rebellion" or personal "outrageous act" may have far-reaching effects on people one will never know. When Rosa Parks sat down on that bus so many years ago, because she was tired from cleaning other people's homes, she had no idea that her one small act would change the world. Dropping a pebble into an ocean can create waves on the other side of the world about which one may never know.

Clients must be taught, by model, by example, by information and inspiration that each action a person takes has a rippling effect in the world. If each of us, therapist and client, is conscious of our actions, big or small, and does things to heal ourselves and others, the world will be better for future generations in ways we may never know. Any positive action taken anywhere will improve the lives of many. The therapy process is an excellent way to provide clients with the tools for change.

REFERENCES

Feminist Therapy Institute, Inc. (1987). *Feminist therapy code of ethics and ethical guidelines for feminist therapists.* Denver: Author.

Greenspan, M. (1983). *A new approach to women and therapy.* New York: McGraw-Hill.

Hanisch, C. (1970). The personal is political. In Firestone, S. and Koedt, A. (Eds.), *Notes from the second year.* New York: Radical Feminists.

Pirke Avot. *Talmud.*

Steinem, G. (1983). *Outrageous acts and everyday rebellions.* New York: Holt, Rinehart, Winston.

Index

Note: Page numbers followed by f indicate figures; page numbers followed by t indicate tables.

© 1998 by The Haworth Press, Inc. All rights reserved.

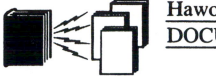

Haworth
DOCUMENT DELIVERY
SERVICE

This valuable service provides a single-article order form for any article from a Haworth journal.

- *Time Saving:* No running around from library to library to find a specific article.
- *Cost Effective:* All costs are kept down to a minimum.
- *Fast Delivery:* Choose from several options, including same-day FAX.
- *No Copyright Hassles:* You will be supplied by the original publisher.
- *Easy Payment:* Choose from several easy payment methods.

Open Accounts Welcome for . . .
- Library Interlibrary Loan Departments
- Library Network/Consortia Wishing to Provide Single-Article Services
- Indexing/Abstracting Services with Single Article Provision Services
- Document Provision Brokers and Freelance Information Service Providers

---

MAIL or *FAX* THIS ENTIRE ORDER FORM TO:

Haworth Document Delivery Service   or FAX: 1-800-895-0582
The Haworth Press, Inc.   or CALL: 1-800-342-9678
10 Alice Street   9am-5pm EST
Binghamton, NY 13904-1580

PLEASE SEND ME PHOTOCOPIES OF THE FOLLOWING SINGLE ARTICLES:

1) Journal Title: _____
    Vol/Issue/Year: _____ Starting & Ending Pages: _____
Article Title: _____

2) Journal Title: _____
    Vol/Issue/Year: _____ Starting & Ending Pages: _____
Article Title: _____

3) Journal Title: _____
    Vol/Issue/Year: _____ Starting & Ending Pages: _____
Article Title: _____

4) Journal Title: _____
    Vol/Issue/Year: _____ Starting & Ending Pages: _____
Article Title: _____

(See other side for Costs and Payment Information)

COSTS: Please figure your cost to order quality copies of an article.

1. Set-up charge per article: $8.00

     ($8.00 × number of separate articles)   _____

2. Photocopying charge for each article:

     1-10 pages: $1.00   _____

     11-19 pages: $3.00   _____

     20-29 pages: $5.00   _____

     30+ pages: $2.00/10 pages   _____

3. Flexicover (optional): $2.00/article   _____

4. Postage & Handling: US: $1.00 for the first article/

     $.50 each additional article   _____

     Federal Express: $25.00   _____

     Outside US: $2.00 for first article/

     $.50 each additional article _____

5. Same-day FAX service: $.35 per page   _____

                    GRAND TOTAL: _____

METHOD OF PAYMENT: (please check one)

❏ Check enclosed   ❏ Please ship and bill. PO # _____

       (sorry we can ship and bill to bookstores only! All others must pre-pay)

❏ Charge to my credit card: ❏ Visa; ❏ MasterCard; ❏ Discover;

          ❏ American Express;

Account Number:_____ Expiration date:_____

Signature: ✗_____

Name: _____ Institution: _____

Address: _____

     _____

City: _____ State:_____ Zip:_____

Phone Number: _____ FAX Number: _____

MAIL or *FAX* THIS ENTIRE ORDER FORM TO:

Haworth Document Delivery Service   **or FAX: 1-800-895-0582**
The Haworth Press, Inc.   **or CALL: 1-800-342-9678**
10 Alice Street   9am-5pm EST)
Binghamton, NY 13904-1580